# Compliance Issues in Gastroenterology

# Compliance Issues in Gastroenterology

EDITED BY

## MICHAEL E. ANDERSON, ESQ

Arent, Fox, Kintner, Plotkin, & Kahn, PLLC
Washington, DC

SLACK
INCORPORATED

*An innovative information, education, and management company*
6900 Grove Road • Thorofare, NJ 08086

Copyright © 2005 by SLACK Incorporated.

ISBN-10: 1-55642-639-9
ISBN-13: 9781556426391

Printed in the United States of America.

Library of Congress Cataloging-in-Publication Data
Compliance issues in gastroenterology / edited by Michael E. Anderson ... [et al.].
   p. ; cm.
  Includes index.
  ISBN 1-55642-639-9 (alk. paper)
  1. Gastroenterology--Practice. 2. Medical laws and legislation.
     [DNLM: 1. Gastroenterology--organization & administration--United States. 2. Insurance Claim Reporting--legislation & jurisprudence--United States. 3. Guideline Adherence--United States. 4. Insurance, Health, Reimbursement--legislation & jurisprudence--United States. 5. Practice Management, Medical--legislation & jurisprudence--United States. WI 33 AA1 C737 2005] I. Anderson, Michael E.

RC801.C645 2005
616.3'3'0068--dc22

                              2004014669

Published by:       SLACK Incorporated
                    6900 Grove Road
                    Thorofare, NJ 08086 USA
                    Telephone: 856-848-1000
                    Fax: 856-853-5991
                    www.slackbooks.com

Contact SLACK Incorporated for more information about other books in this field or about the availability of our books from distributors outside the United States.

Last digit is print number: 10   9   8   7   6   5   4   3   2   1

# CONTENTS

# EDITOR AND CONTRIBUTING AUTHOR

*Michael E. Anderson, JD* is a partner in the Washington, DC office of Arent Fox PLLC, and is a member of the firm's Health Law Practice Group. Mr. Anderson concentrates his practice in the areas of health care counseling and litigation, with particular emphasis on transactional and regulatory counseling, Medicare and Medicaid reimbursement, and fraud and abuse counseling (including the civil and criminal defense of fraud-related allegations, the conducting of internal investigations, and the development and implementation of corporate compliance programs).

He serves as outside counsel to a variety of health care entities, including academic and community-based general and specialty hospitals, individual and group-based physician practices, clinical laboratories, diagnostic clinics, ambulatory surgical centers, pharmaceutical and medical device manufacturers, and the like. Mr. Anderson provides counseling on such matters as federal and state regulation, reimbursement, fraud and abuse issues, organization finances, internal governance/structure issues, medical staff matters, resource contracting, and research-related concerns such as patient rights issues, research protocols, and grant proposal development.

Mr. Anderson is a member of the Fraud and Abuse, Self-Referrals, and False Claims Committee; the Physician Organizations Committee; and the Long Term Care Substantive Law Committee, all through the American Health Lawyers Association. Additionally, Mr. Anderson sits on the Health Care Contracting Committee and the Procurement Fraud Committee, both through the American Bar Association's (ABA) Section of Public Contract Law, as well as the Health Law Litigation Committee of the ABA's Section of Litigation, and the ABA's Health Law Section.

Mr. Anderson is a frequent speaker and author on a variety of health care topics and has written several books on health care related compliance issues. He also authors a monthly legal update column for the magazine *Assisted Living Today* and regularly contributes to various other health care publications.

# CONTRIBUTING AUTHORS

*Emily Hill, PA-C* has more than 12 years of experience as a health care consultant working with numerous academic and private practices on coding, reimbursement, and compliance issues. Ms. Hill has taught coding courses for numerous specialty societies, health systems, and medical practices. She currently serves on the American Medical Association's Correct Coding Committee, the Health Care Professionals Advisory Committee, and the National Uniform Claim Committee. She is a graduate of the University of North Carolina at Chapel Hill and Wake Forest University School of Medicine Physician Assistant Program.

*Daniel L. Johnson, CPC, CPC-H* is a Senior Consultant with MAG Mutual Healthcare Solutions, Inc. He has more than 21 years of experience in health care that includes clinical experience, regulatory compliance, health care policy analysis, and medical management. Mr. Johnson has experience in the administration of corporate integrity agreements between health care providers and the federal government; physician representation involving Medicare and third-party payer audits and, with attorney guidance, against fraud and abuse allegations; and the conducting of compliance risk assessments for physicians and other health care providers. Mr. Johnson also serves as a Compliance Officer for physician practices and provides consulting advice to physicians and their staffs on reimbursement issues, fee schedule analysis, Medicare audit defense, coding and regulatory compliance, and HIPAA. He also performs medical practice evaluations and assists with managed care contract negotiations.

*Alan E. Reider, MPH, JD* is a partner in the Washington, DC office of Arent Fox and is a member of the firm's Health Law Practice Group. He represents national health care corporations, as well as institutional providers and individual practitioners and suppliers. His representation focuses on regulatory issues involving federal programs including reimbursement, coverage, and certification, as well as relationships with third party payers and counseling in the area of fraud and abuse, principally the Federal Anti-Kickback and Stark self-referral laws. Mr. Reider has served as lead defense counsel in several government investigation cases, including National Medical Care, at the time the largest health care fraud case in history. He has defended hospitals, physicians, ambulatory surgery centers, suppliers, and pharmaceutical companies in government enforcement actions. He also served as one of the principal defense lawyers in the landmark National Health Laboratories settlement, the first major health care False Claims Act case. Mr. Reider's work in the compliance area extends to all parts of the health care industry. He has developed Compliance Programs for large national health care companies and individual providers, including hospitals, nursing homes, suppliers, and physician practices. He has published model compliance documents for national physician professional societies, and assisted in the development of marketing guidelines for national pharmaceutical and medical device companies.

*Allison Weber Shuren, MSN, JD* is an associate with Arent Fox in Washington. She focuses her practice on regulatory and legislative health care matters involving corporate compliance program implementation and review; Medicare coverage, reimbursement, and overpayment matters; fraud and abuse counseling and investigations, including issues related to sales and marketing practices; False Claims Act defense; industry-sponsored and federally-funded human subject research compliance; the HIPAA Privacy Standards; joint venture transactions; and issues related to telemedicine and e-health. She advises a diverse group of clients, including hospitals and academic medical centers, physician practices, ambulatory surgery centers, diagnostic imaging centers, health care professional societies, pharmaceutical and medical device companies, and internet-based health care companies.

*Jo-Ann Marchica, JD* is an associate in the New York office of Arent Fox, concentrating on regulatory matters related to health and corporate transactions. She has represented a variety of health care clients, including long-term care and post-acute care providers, physicians, managed care organizations, and durable medical equipment providers. Her health care practice focuses on advising clients on regulatory, licensing, and certificate of need matters; anti-kick-back, self-referral, and corporate practice of medicine issues; as well as Medicare and Medicaid reimbursement issues.

*Lorie A. Mayorga, JD* is an associate in the Washington, DC office of Arent Fox. She has focused her practice on federal health care program reimbursement issues, providing advice and performing federal litigation as well as representing health care clients before agencies in adversarial and nonadversarial proceedings. She has counseled for-profit and tax-exempt hospital systems, skilled nursing facilities, medical equipment suppliers, home health agencies, hospices, ambulatory surgical centers, outpatient therapy providers, and physician groups on compliance with federal regulations, on Medicare, Medicaid and TRICARE reimbursement rules, and on the implications of both for proposed transactions. Before coming to Arent Fox, Ms. Mayorga spent 6 years working in the Department of Health and Human Services, primarily for the Office of General Counsel division responsible for the Centers for Medicare and Medicaid Services where she specialized in Medicare inpatient hospital reimbursement litigation.

*Eileen L. Kahaner, JD* practices with the Health Care Group in the Washington, DC office of Sidley & Austin. She has experience counseling health care providers on state and federal fraud and abuse, regulatory, HIPAA, transactional, and corporate compliance matters. She also has advised clients involved in Medicare and Medicaid audits and False Claims Act investigations. Ms. Kahaner regularly advises clients regarding regulatory compliance issues and assists them in designing and implementing their corporate compliance programs. In addition, on behalf of providers subject to federal investigation, she has negotiated corporate integrity agreements with the Office of the Inspector General of the Department of Health and Human Services.

*Anthony T. Pavel, JD* is an attorney with Kirkpatrick and Lockhart in Washington. His practice focuses on e-health and telemedicine, credentialing, and regulatory and legislative health care issues. He also works on matters concerning corporate compliance, Medicare and Medicaid reimbursement, fraud and abuse, practitioner reimbursement, and health insurance.

# INTRODUCTION

It certainly comes as no surprise to physicians that today's health care fraud enforcement environment is very different from that of even a few years ago. The amount of resources dedicated to fraud enforcement activities has grown dramatically each year since 1992. Civil actions and criminal prosecutions initiated by the US Department of Justice have increased sharply. On the criminal side, prosecutors commonly allege mail fraud, payments of kickbacks, money laundering, the filing of false claims, and conspiracy to defraud the government as illegal activities engaged in by physicians. On the civil side, the government's principal tool has been the federal False Claims Act, under which it can recover triple the actual damages incurred by the government as a result of the false claim, plus a penalty of up to $10,000 for each fraudulent request for reimbursement. Having said this, however, the government's current enforcement philosophy stresses an emphasis on proper business conduct by physicians in an effort to prevent health care fraud in the first place. This is why compliance programs have become so important: their goal is to prevent violations of law, or if violations do occur, to afford a mechanism to effectively rectify the problem and, if necessary, inform the government.

As one might expect, this increasingly aggressive level of enforcement activity has caused physicians to focus more keenly on the way they bill for their services and otherwise handle the business side of their practice. Regardless of the size of the practice, there are a seemingly infinite number of rules and regulations involved in the business of medicine. Every physician strives to comply with these rules in order to ensure that he or she is practicing within the boundaries of the law. However, with those boundaries sometimes difficult to define given the complexity of today's health care laws, how is a physician to accurately determine what conduct and practices are safely within those boundaries?

This book will not provide the answers to all of the questions that face gastroenterologists in their search for the exact boundaries of permissible conduct. If it fulfills its mission however, it will provide information about some of the more common billing and legal issues that face gastroenterology practices today and will provide advice on how to address those issues. Physicians are cautioned: the information in this book does not constitute legal or coding advice. It simply serves to alert gastroenterologists to issues that may be applicable to them. Any specific questions should be directed to one's attorney or coding specialist.

The team of contributing authors assembled to write this book have extensive experience with compliance issues related to physician practices generally and to gastroenterology practices in particular. Each of us has enormous respect for the field and for the physicians and other health care professionals with whom we have had the privilege of working. This book reflects a compilation of some of the issues we have identified during the course of our work. If every reader finds at least one issue that applies to his or her practice and which helps to bring that practice closer to full compliance, then we will consider the hours spent developing this book to have been most worthwhile.

*Michael E. Anderson*
*Washington, DC*

# BILLING ISSUES

# CLAIMS PROCESSING SOFTWARE

A gastroenterology practice has continuing problems with its claims submissions, and experiences significant denials by the Medicare carrier and private insurers. Its physicians are rushed and do not fill out their superbills completely, the billing department has been suffering from constant turnover, its billing staff is inexperienced and untrained, and the local Medicare carrier is constantly changing its policies and tightening its systems. In a professional society meeting, the physicians are attracted to an exhibitor promoting claims processing software. Marketed as "the closest thing to being idiot proof," the software is designed to minimize all of the problems the physicians have been facing. One function, which is particularly intriguing, includes a default system that will automatically reject any diagnosis code which does not support the procedure billed and replace it with the most common code used by physicians for the particular procedure. The physicians think this may be the answer they have been looking for.

## CAN THIS SOFTWARE PACKAGE SOLVE THE GASTROENTEROLOGISTS' PROBLEMS?

While this software billing package may solve the doctors' problems with excessive denials, it would create a far bigger one: the risk of filing false claims. When a claim is submitted for reimbursement, it is not only a statement of what was done (through the Current Procedural Terminology [CPT] Code), but is also a statement of why a service was performed (through the ICD-9 [International Classification of Diseases] Code). Only the physician is in a position to state why a particular procedure or service was performed. If the software program changes an ICD-9 code entered by the physician to a code that will ensure that the claim will be paid, the government likely will take the position that the physician has caused a false claim to be submitted and could subject the practice to treble damages and penalties.

The concept of manipulating the ICD-9 code to assure that a claim is paid has been described as "code steering" or "code stuffing." In the mid-1990s, there were a series of federal investigations of clinical laboratories that were accused of advising physicians on which codes should be used in order to assure reimbursement of clinical laboratory services (code steering), as well as cases where physicians used the "wrong" code or no code, in which case the laboratory would file the claim using a code designed to assure payment (code stuffing). Each of these investigations resulted in significant settlement payments by the laboratories. Physicians who employ software that manipulates the ICD-9 code to assure payment would be subject to similar risk of False Claims Act liability.

## MISIDENTIFICATION OF THE PROVIDER

A group of gastroenterologists added a physician to their practice. The new physician was just out of a residency program and had not been practicing in the state. An application for a Medicare provider number was submitted, but was pending approval. Applications for other health plans also were pending. For the purpose of reimbursement, it was decided that the new physician's services would temporarily be billed under another physician's name and personal identification number (PIN). This physician would not render the service, but would co-sign the new physician's charts.

### IS THIS PROCESS ACCEPTABLE TO
### MEDICARE AND OTHER PAYERS?

This process is not acceptable under Medicare requirements or by most other insurance companies. Unless instructed differently by a payer in writing, each physician in a group practice must apply for and maintain his or her own identification number. That number must be reflected on the claim form to identify who provided the service.

By way of example, one Medicare carrier addresses the issue of improper use of another physician's PIN as follows:

> "Medicare is also aware that some groups or entities are submitting claims for the new physicians or nonphysician practitioners using one of the other physician's Medicare Provider Identification Numbers while waiting for the new PIN to be issued. This is not acceptable practice. Before these services can be billed to Medicare, each provider must obtain his or her own PIN. The claims for that provider should be held until Medicare issues a PIN number."

It is important to recognize that the delay in obtaining a PIN will not likely impact the ability of the physician or practice to be paid for the services. The Medicare program, and most insurers, will accept claims for services rendered as of the date the request for a PIN has been submitted. Thus, while awaiting the issuance of a PIN may create temporary cash flow problems, it should not adversely affect payment. On the other hand, to use an incorrect PIN to obtain payment is likely to result in allegations that an improper claim was submitted. Such violations carry potentially severe penalties under state and federal law.

# New Patient for the Physician or New Patient for the Practice?

A physician joins a new group practice and does not bring patient medical records from his prior practice. One of the physician's prior, established patients is scheduled in the new practice for a follow-up of irritable bowel syndrome. Prior to the examination, a new patient chart is created, medical history obtained, patient demographic information form completed, and lifetime signature statement obtained.

## Is this Service Considered an Established Patient Visit or May a New Patient Visit be Billed?

Medicare interprets the phrase "new patient" to mean a patient who has not received any professional services from the physician within the previous 3 years.

Therefore, if the patient were seen by the same physician in the prior practice within the past 3 years, a new patient examination would not be appropriate. In this case, the physician may bill a level of established office visit code to reflect the time and effort necessary to review the patient's medical history, data and tests, and physical examination required since this information was not available to the new practice.

However, had the patient received only technical services such as interpretation of diagnostic tests and had no face-to-face encounter with the physician in the last 3 years, then the "new patient" visit may be coded. Technical services do not constitute "physician professional services," and documentation of these types of services in the patient chart would not prohibit a physician from billing a new patient examination.

# 4

## USE OF SCRIBES TO COMPLETE SUPERBILL

A large gastroenterology practice (the "Practice") uses a scribe system to speed the documentation process and improve patient flow. It is the policy of the Practice for scribes to fill out the history and physical examination form, the progress notes, and the charge form including entering the ICD-9 and CPT codes. During an audit of the Practice's documentation system, the compliance officer discovered that many of the physicians sign the scribe's notes and the charge form without verifying that the content of the forms is correct. At the next medical staff meeting, the compliance officer advises the physicians that they must review the information in the medical record and on the charge form for accuracy before affixing their signature because the government will hold them accountable for the content. The physicians argue that it is the scribes' responsibility to ensure the information is correct, not theirs.

## WHO IS CORRECT, THE PHYSICIANS OR THE COMPLIANCE OFFICER?

The compliance officer. The documentation in a patient's medical record and on a charge form is a confirmation of the physician's decision regarding the services ordered, the services performed, and the clinical basis for ordering those services. In its *Compliance Program Guidance for Individual and Small Group Practice Physician Practices*, the Office of the Inspector General (OIG) made clear that health care providers have a duty to reasonably ensure that claims submitted for their services to any federally-funded health care programs are true and accurate (65 Fed. Reg. 59434 [Oct. 5, 2000]). The OIG also explained that the CPT and ICD-9 codes reported on health insurance claims forms must be supported by the medical record, and that the record should contain all necessary information to validate: (1) the site of service, (2) the appropriateness of the services provided, (3) the accuracy of the billing, and (4) the identity of the caregiver.

In a situation where a scribe fails to select the appropriate procedure or diagnosis codes or fails to document services correctly, such as under the facts described above, the government could take the position that the Practice physicians acted recklessly within the meaning of the Federal Civil False Claims Act by delegating their responsibility for documentation and coding to nonclinicians and not reviewing the scribe's decisions. In order for the Practice to manage its risk under the False Claims Act, the physicians either must complete all documentation, or at a minimum, the physicians must review the scribes' medical record entries and code selections to ensure that they are correct.

# BILLING FOR CONSULTATIONS WITHIN A GROUP PRACTICE

An internist sees a patient for an annual physical examination. The patient complains of alternating constipation and diarrhea and lower abdominal pain after eating. The abdominal examination reveals distinct tenderness in the right lower quadrant and mild discomfort throughout the lower abdominal area. The hemoccult examination was negative. The internist suggests that the patient see a gastroenterologist within the group. The plan entry in the patient's chart indicates: "Referred to gastroenterologist for evaluation of GI complaints and possible colonoscopy. Return in 1 year for annual examination or as needed."

Upon returning to the front desk to schedule the GI appointment, the patient learns that the gastroenterologist has had an appointment cancellation and is available immediately. A medical assistant leads the patient back to the GI physician's examination room.

The medical assistant indicates in the subjective entry of the chart: "Referred by Dr. X for evaluation of abdominal pain and alternating diarrhea/constipation and possible colonoscopy." The gastroenterologist reviews the internist's notes, obtains additional history, and performs an abdominal and rectal examination. After discussion with the patient, a colonoscopy is scheduled for the following week. The medical assistant reviews instructions with the patient.

The patient chart is then returned to the internist to review the findings and recommendations. The internist initials the notes in the patient's chart as read.

## IS THE INTRAOFFICE CONSULTATION BILLABLE?

One of the most common billing errors in gastroenterology is the failure to bill for intraoffice consultations within a group practice.

Referrals for evaluation between two different specialty trained physicians within the same clinic can establish the basis for a consultation. The documentation required to support an intraoffice consultation is the same as a regular consultation, with the exception that a separate written report, beyond the consultant's entry in the practice's medical record, does not need to be furnished to the referring physician.

The consultant's report that is already a part of the patient's medical record can serve as the written report of findings. It is recommended that the referring physician review and initial the findings.

Caution should be taken when billing level of service for intraoffice consultations. Since the patient has already been examined by another physician and is being referred for a specific problem within the GI system, the level of service might be limited by the extent of the history and examination that is necessary to evaluate the patient. In some cases, it might be beneficial to select the level of service based on time spent counseling the patient rather than the content of the history, examination, and medical decision-making (see Chapter 10, Using Time to Bill Evaluation and Management Services).

The level of service billed must comply with all the documentation requirements of history, examination, and medical decision-making or the use of time. There also must be documented evidence of the need for the level of service billed, which will be based on the nature of the patient's presenting problem.

# MULTIPLE ENDOSCOPIC PROCEDURES

A patient presents at Dr. Williams' office with hematochezia. Dr. Williams performs an upper gastrointestinal endoscopy but the source of the blood is not discovered. Dr. Williams then performs a colonoscopy with polypectomy by snare. The patient is discharged but comes back to Dr. Williams' office later that same day complaining of rectal bleeding. Dr. Williams performs a second colonoscopy to recauterize the site of the removed polyp.

## HOW DOES DR. WILLIAMS PROPERLY BILL FOR THESE MULTIPLE PROCEDURES?

Under Medicare, two different rules would be applied to determine appropriate reimbursement for multiple endoscopic procedures.

First, the "standard rule for multiple surgeries" provides that if two or more procedures with *different* endoscopic base codes are performed on the same day, the procedures should be listed on the claim in descending order according to their relative value units (RVUs). Medicare will then reimburse at full value the procedure with the highest RVU and at 50% of the value of the usual fee for the other procedures. Medicare further provides that the multiple procedures modifier –51 should be used with the lesser-valued surgical procedures, although this is not uniformly required by all local Medicare payers.

Secondly, the "special payment rule for multiple endoscopies" provides that if two or more procedures with the same endoscopic base code are performed on the same day, as with the standard rule, the procedures should be listed on the claim in descending order according to the RVU. Medicare will then reimburse at full value the procedures with the highest RVU and reimburse the other procedures at their value, less the value of their endoscopic base codes.

Such multiple procedures from related endoscopic families should use the modifier –59, if bundled in the Correct Coding Initiative, or modifier –51 if not bundled.

# 7

A patient presents to the physician with a complaint of severe difficulty swallowing. The patient has had previous esophageal dilations for strictures. Based on the patient's history and current complaints, a dilation of the esophagus is planned. The dilation is performed later the same day at the hospital's outpatient department.

## MAY THE PHYSICIAN BILL FOR THE EXAMINATION PERFORMED ON THE SAME DAY AS THE PROCEDURE?

Evaluation and Management (E/M) services by the same physician on the day of a procedure can be reported if they are significant and separately identifiable from the procedure. This means that the E/M services provided are above and beyond the typical pre- and postprocedure care provided in conjunction with the procedure.

In general, both the E/M service and the procedure are reported if the decision to perform the procedure was made at the same encounter as the E/M service. According to CPT and Medicare guidelines, the E/M service may be initiated by the symptom or condition for which the procedure was performed. Therefore, different diagnoses are not required in these instances. Both services would also be reported if the E/M service was for one diagnosis and the procedure was performed for a different reason.

In the case above, the visit on the day of the procedure was properly documented as the visit to determine the need for the procedure. Therefore, the visit may be billed to Medicare with a –25 modifier, reflecting a significant, separately identifiable E/M service on the same day as the procedure.

# 8

## BUNDLING

In September 2002, a gastroenterologist received a request from Medicare for copies of medical records supporting previously paid claims for codes 44397 (colonoscopy through stoma, with transendoscopic stent placement) and 44391 (colonoscopy through stoma with control of bleeding). The charts requested were for services rendered over a 5-month period in 2001. The audit resulted in denials for the services and an overpayment request. In the opinion of Medicare's reviewer, the charge for 44391 was unjustified and should have been denied as an incidental component of the stent placement (ie, bundled under the national Correct Coding Initiative [CCI]).

### WAS THE MEDICARE CARRIER DETERMINATION ACCURATE?

The Center for Medicare and Medicaid Services (CMS) developed the national CCI to promote correct coding methodologies. CCI edits are based on coding conventions defined in the AMA's *CPT Manual*, current standards of medical and surgical coding practice, input from specialty societies, and analysis of current coding practices. The edits are updated quarterly with an effective date of the first of every quarter (ie, January 1, April 1, July 1, and October 1).

It is important to note that the edits are not retroactive, but effective from the designated date. This means that the CCI limitations may only be applied prospectively.

In this case, the Medicare reviewer applied current CCI edits retroactively to prior dates of service. Specifically, 44391 was not bundled with 44397 until July 1, 2002. As a result, the gastroenterologist objected to the denials by pursuing an appeal to a carrier Hearing Officer. On the basis of the improper retroactive application of the CCI edit, the Hearing Officer reversed the denial and overpayment determination.

Even if a combination of codes are subject to CCI edits, the CCI permits both services to be reported if the services are distinct or independent of each other. Modifier −59 should be used in these situations.

A practice decides that it does not want to make contractual adjustments after receiving payments from its various payers (a contractual adjustment is the write-off that a practice takes after it is paid by a payer to reflect the difference between the provider's charges and the allowable that has been paid). Accordingly, the practice abandons its single fee schedule and develops one that, for each payer, makes the applicable charge what that payer will accept as the maximum allowable. Because the practice is located in an area where there is a heavy penetration of managed care providers, charges for 54 percent of the practice's patients under this system will be significantly lower than the Medicare allowable for the service.

## MAY THE PRACTICE BILL FOR
## NON-MEDICARE PATIENTS AT A SIGNIFICANT
## DISCOUNT FROM THE MEDICARE CHARGE?

The Medicare statute contains a prohibition against a physician or provider from charging the Medicare program an amount substantially in excess of the practice's usual charge. The penalty for violating this provision is exclusion from the Medicare and Medicaid programs. Unfortunately, there has been no formal guidance from the OIG or the CMS concerning the standards to apply in determining how much is "substantially in excess," and what constitutes a practice's "usual charge." As a result, practices have had to rely on common sense and the limited informal guidance that has developed over the years.

The more significant issue is what constitutes a practice's "usual charge." It has been generally recognized that the "usual charge" is the amount charged to the practice's typical patient. Thus, if a practice charges a rate to the majority of its patients, it likely would be considered a practice's "usual charge." In this case, however, the majority of the patients are covered by managed care programs. According to informal opinions from the former Health Care Financing Administration, the managed care population is not considered when a practice's "usual charge" is determined. Instead, it appears that the program would limit its consideration to patients who are not covered by managed care programs.

Therefore, in this example, even though the practice's charge to a majority of its patients may be substantially below the Medicare charge, it appears that the statutory prohibition would not be triggered, as long as the charge to non-managed care patients is consistent with the Medicare charge.

With respect to the question of what constitutes "substantially in excess," there is absolutely no guidance. Here common sense must dictate a practice's pricing decisions. Clearly, if Medicare were charged a premium above all other payers, the government undoubtedly would view such conduct unfavorably and would argue that even a modest premium could constitute "substantially in excess." On the other hand, if the practice's charges varied widely, and there were no "Medicare premium" pricing, such a position would be less likely.

# Using Time to Bill Evaluation and Management Services

A gastroenterologist is meeting with a patient newly diagnosed with Crohn's disease. The patient presents to discuss treatment options with the gastroenterologist. Although the physician performs a brief history and examination, most of the 25 minutes the physician spends face-to-face with the patient involve a discussion of treatment options and coordinating the initiation of steroid therapy. Follow-up visits and monitoring also are recommended. From a documentation standpoint, the patient encounter would meet a level 2-3 established patient office visit.

## Is a More Extensive Evaluation and Management Service Billable?

Typically, the extent of history, examination, and medical decision-making elements found in the patient's medical record dictate the level of care billed. However, the AMA's *CPT Manual* and CMS' *Documentation Guidelines* recognize another method for coding evaluation and management services based upon the time spent in counseling or coordinating care.

CPT and Medicare's *Documentation Guidelines* permit coding a visit using time if greater than 50% of the patient encounter is spent in face-to-face counseling. Counseling is defined as "a discussion with a patient and/or family concerning one or more of the following areas:

- Diagnostic results, impressions, and/or recommended diagnostic studies.
- Prognosis.
- Risks and benefits of management (treatment) options.
- Instructions for management (treatment) options.

- Importance of compliance with chosen management (treatment) options.
- Risk factor reduction.
- Patient and family education.

If the gastroenterologist spent at least 15 minutes involved in counseling and care coordination, the visit may be coded as a level 3 E/M service (eg, 99213). The physician should document the total length of time (as defined by CPT) of the encounter and the record should describe the counseling and/or activities to coordinate care. The time spent counseling and total face-to-face time by the physician also should be estimated and documented.

Most CPT E/M codes, with the exception of Emergency Department services, have typical patient encounter times. Refer to these times for appropriate coding and billing.

# BILLING FOR TELEPHONE CALLS AND E-MAILS

Dr. Johnson, a very conscientious gastroenterologist, prides himself on his "bedside manner." He believes the one-on-one relationship between patient and physician is very important and therefore tries to always make himself available for phone calls from patients with questions or who just need to talk over their concerns. He is very generous with his time and tries to give patients all the time they need to address an issue. The problem is, Dr. Johnson also has a very busy practice and has noted recently that in an average week the time he spends on the phone with patients and responding to patient e-mails amounts to 6 to 8 hours or so. In an attempt to maintain his practice standards yet be fairer to his bottom line, Dr. Johnson has decided to start billing the patients' insurance companies for these phone calls, though he has no intention of actually ever billing patients in the event the insurance company doesn't pay.

## IS THIS A SOUND BILLING PRACTICE?

While *some* insurance companies will pay for telephone calls between physician and patient, most will not, following the Medicare rule that such calls are deemed "noncovered services." So to the extent Dr. Johnson can identify those payers who will reimburse for the calls (CPTs 99371-99373) or e-mails (CPT 99499), then billing would be appropriate, provided, however, that he is prepared to bill the patient if for some reason a company who says it *will* reimburse for the calls doesn't.

"Blanket billing" of all insurance companies in hopes that some will pay, followed by a write-off of the charges for those who don't is *not* recommended, however. If the physician never intends to actually bill the patient for the service in the event the claim for reimbursement is denied by the payer, then the insurance company will view the physician's bill as invalid and could well pursue the submission for reimbursement as a fraudulent claim. If you choose to bill an insurance company for a service, you are obligated to bill the patient if the insurance company ultimately rejects the claim for any reason (unless, of course, your contract with the payer prevents patient billing).

# ARGON PLASMA COAGULATION

A suburban gastroenterology practice recently began using argon plasma coagulation (APC) primarily to treat AV malformations in the colon, but is less than clear on how to appropriately bill for a procedure that utilizes APC.

## WHAT ARE THE GUIDELINES FOR BILLING FOR PROCEDURES USING ARGON PLASMA COAGULATION?

While the answer may seem obvious on its face, this is an example of a problem that often keeps practices searching in vain for the right code. The key is to focus first on the end result—*what the physician actually did during the procedure*—rather than the equipment, instrument, or device utilized. The APC can be used in a variety of gastrointestinal procedures to both control bleeding and destroy tissue. While both of these objectives may be a part of a procedure to treat AV malformations, the APC is also commonly used in treating strictures, sessile polyps, and the like. Again, the key for proper coding is to look to the procedure utilizing the equipment or instrument and the clinical objectives of that *procedure* rather than the use of the equipment, instrument, or device itself.

# 13

## PROPER BILLING FOR THE SERVICES OF A NUTRITIONIST

A gastroenterology practice employs a full-time nutritionist to help better serve the digestive health needs of its patients. May the practice bill Medicare for the services provided by the nutritionist?

### "INCIDENT TO" BILLING

The general rule under Medicare is that only the person providing the service can bill for the service. However, an exception to the general rule exists when services are furnished "incident to a physician's professional service." In such case, the services may be performed by someone other than the billing physician (such as a nutritionist) if the following criteria are met:

- The service is provided in a physician's office. Services provided in any other location (eg, hospital, ambulatory surgery center [ASC], nursing home, etc.) would not qualify as billable by the physician unless personally performed by the physician.
- The service must be directly supervised by the billing physician. Direct supervision requires that the billing physician be in the office suite (not necessarily the exam room with the patient) when the service is provided.
- The person providing the service must be an employee of the physician or the group under which the billing physician is employed or contracted.
- The service provided is an integral, although incidental, part of the physician's professional service. The billing physician or another physician in the group must have seen and evaluated the patient prior to the provision of the "incident to" service. Nonphysician providers cannot provide a service to a new patient and bill that service under the supervising physician's name and provider number.

Hence, provided the above criteria are met, it would be appropriate for the practice to bill for the nutritionist's services as incident to the physician's professional service.

# BILLING FOR NEW TECHNOLOGY

A gastroenterologist and a colleague discussed emerging techniques and technology used to treat colon polyps. Both agreed that the benefits of the technology appeared to offer significant advantages over existing technology. The colleague mentioned that an existing CPT code appeared to describe these procedures and encouraged billing with this code. The gastroenterologist was enthused by what he heard and verified the coding and reimbursement with a vendor. The vendor assured him that the existing CPT code could be used to bill for these procedures. The gastroenterologist purchased the instruments and began treating patients, and billing for his services.

## AN ISSUE OF PAYMENT

The problem with this common scenario is that no one bothered to confirm that the service would be covered by payers. The fact that an apparently applicable CPT code exists does not automatically guarantee payment. In this case, the "new" technology might be deemed unproven, experimental, or investigational by third-party payers. Payers generally are suspicious of new procedures with an unproven track record or expensive costs. Payment for such procedures is customarily the patient's responsibility. Under Medicare's program standards, investigational procedures are not covered.

Even if the claim was initially paid, if the payer later discovers that the service involved a new technology, there is a risk that any paid claims may subsequently be reversed and subject to a refund. Any pending claims also would then be denied.

## RESOLUTION

Before investing resources in new technology, the physician should have investigated the coding and payment rules of the carriers to which he most frequently submits claims, in addition to treatment options and patient satisfaction outcomes. Communication with the payers should be done in writing. If no rules exist, it does not necessarily mean that the physician should refrain from investing in this new technology, but that the opportunities for payment may be limited.

If no specific CPT code exists for the service or procedure, the CPT manual states that an unlisted code should be used. The physician should not file the claim electronically, so that an individual at the payer has the opportunity to manually review the claim and any supporting documentation. In addition, if the physician believes he has identified patients who may benefit from the new procedure, he should inform the patients in advance that the service might not be covered. Before the procedure is performed, the patient should accept financial responsibility by signing an Advanced Beneficiary Notice (ABN) or similar document.

Involving specialty societies early and often is critical if billing and reimbursement for new technology is to be successful. It takes approximately 2 years for a new CPT code to be created, in the event a new CPT code is required. Even after a CPT code is established, continuing discussions with the payers must occur in order to assign relative value units (done by the American Medical Association [AMA] and Medicare) and establish reimbursement rates.

# 15

## WORKING WITH RADIOLOGISTS

Advances in imaging technology have moved a number of specialties, including gastroenterology, into the traditional realm of radiology. Can a gastroenterologist bill for guiding an imaging device if she is not going to interpret the results? What about billing for a technically similar procedure in which the gastroenterologist's only involvement is interpreting the results?

Fortunately, the procedural terminology allows for the overlapping "technical" and "professional" competencies of gastroenterologists with radiologists, nuclear medicine physicians, surgeons, and others. If a physician performs a test but does not interpret the results, she adds the modifier "TC" to the procedure code to indicate that she performed the technical component. On the other hand, if a gastroenterologist interprets a CT scan performed by someone else, he uses the modifier "26" to claim payment only for the professional component of the procedure. If the technical component is performed by an outside radiologist or technician as a purchased service, for which the gastroenterologist is going to bill the payer, the technical component must appear as a separate item with the modifier "WU" and include identifying information about the supplier and how much the test cost. (If a gastroenterologist interprets the results of a test performed by his employee, he can bill globally for the procedure as if he had performed both components himself.)

Gastroenterologists and their patients can benefit greatly from a cooperative relationship with an experienced radiologist. In the case of intermittent symptoms, a radiologist who is willing to arrange to see a patient on an urgent basis when an episode occurs can make it possible to diagnose a stricture that may have been missed by years of radiographs taken between episodes. Also, a radiologist familiar with intestinal x-rays will keep a close eye on the patient and the films as the barium progresses, so that he can recognize the narrowing as soon as the barium reaches it, instead of trying to make observations after overlapping loops of intestine have filled with barium and blocked the scene. If a practice can find, or develop, a gastrointestinal radiologist, the availability of superior results from inexpensive tests will enhance everything from patient outcomes to credibility with payers.

# Advanced Beneficiary Notices

Gastroenterology Specialists ("GS") offers a particular diagnostic test to certain patients, and while the physicians in the group believe the test is medically necessary for this patient population, the Medicare carrier generally denies payment for the service. There is no National Coverage Determination regarding the test, nor a Local Medical Review Policy. In order to protect itself, GS requires every Medicare beneficiary who wants to undergo the study to sign an Advanced Beneficiary Notice (ABN) informing the patient that Medicare may deny payment for the test on the grounds that it was not medically necessary, and that if Medicare should refuse coverage, the patient is responsible for paying the fee for the test.

## Is this a Proper Use of an Advanced Beneficiary Notice?

Medicare protects beneficiaries from liability for claims that are denied because the medical care is deemed to be not medically necessary, if the beneficiary did not know, and had no reason to know the care was not medically necessary.

In deciding whether a beneficiary knew or reasonably could be expected to have known that an item or service he or she received was not reasonable and necessary, Medicare carriers will accept a beneficiary's allegation that he or she did not know in the absence of evidence that rebuts the beneficiary's position. ABNs are forms that allow a physician to document that a beneficiary was informed in writing that Medicare likely would not pay for an item or service before the service was furnished, and that the beneficiary agreed to pay for the physician for the service.

To be considered adequate notice, an ABN must: (1) be provided to the patient *prior to when the excluded item or service is performed*, (2) describe the particular service(s) involved, and (3) contain the physician's reasons for believing Medicare will deny payment.

Because an ABN must describe the item or service and the reason for the expected denial with some specificity, the requirement for advanced notice is not satisfied by a signed statement that states only that there is a possibility that Medicare may not pay for the service or where a physician routinely gives such notice to all beneficiaries for whom the physician provides services or classes of services.

In the situation described above, GS reasonably could be expected to know that the carrier will deny payment for the diagnostic test at issue. Therefore, in order to shift liability for the cost of the test from GS to the patient benefiting from the test, GS must provide an ABN to each patient for whom the test is recommended before furnishing the test. To be certain it provides sufficient notice, GS should use the ABN developed and approved by the CMS for use with Part B services.

# Confirming Carrier Coding Advice

There is a difference of opinion within a large gastroenterology practice on a coding question. The practice administrator brings the question to the compliance officer. The compliance officer believes that the practice codes the service appropriately, but wants to make certain of that fact. Accordingly, the compliance officer contacts the carrier and asks the question. On the phone, the carrier representative confirms that the practice's current understanding of the coding criteria is correct. The compliance officer calls the practice administrator and tells him to continue as before, that the carrier has confirmed the practice's current use of the code.

## Is Telephone Advice From The Carrier Adequate To Protect The Practice?

At first glance, the administrator and the compliance officer have done everything correctly to protect the practice. Being uncertain about a compliance issue, the practice contacted the carrier and confirmed the actions. This should, one would expect, ensure that: (1) the practice is acting on correct guidance, and (2) if the advice were incorrect, the practice's reliance on the carrier would protect the practice if enforcement authorities question the practice's policies or billings. Unfortunately, neither expectation is necessarily the case. Because carriers do not always interpret the Medicare requirements correctly or the same as CMS, there is no guarantee that the carrier advice is correct. However, there are several things a practice can do to minimize its exposure in such cases. The key is documentation. Appropriate documentation will help establish that the practice's reliance on the carrier advice was reasonable.

In its *Compliance Program Guidance for Individual and Small Group Physician Practices* (see Chapter 49), the OIG recommends that physician practices *document* efforts to comply with applicable federal health care program requirements. The OIG suggests that practices document and retain records of requests and any written or oral responses. This step is extremely important if the practice intends to rely on that response to guide it in future decisions, actions, or reimbursement requests. A written inquiry with a written response is preferred and should be obtained whenever possible.

If, for some reason, written confirmation is not possible, the practice should take steps to protect itself. The OIG has suggested that a practice maintain a log of oral inquiries between the practice and carrier representatives. The log should include the date of the call, the phone number called, the name (first and last) of the person at the carrier to whom you spoke, the question asked, and the answer (as close to verbatim as possible). In addition, the practice should write a letter to the carrier, stating the oral advice received and the practice's intention to rely on the advice. The letter should request that the carrier advise the practice if the practice's understanding is incorrect. Such documentation should help protect the practice should the carrier representative's oral advice turn out to be incorrect.

# Interpretation and Reports for Diagnostic Tests

A patient presents for an evaluation of difficulty swallowing and inability to eat normal quantities of food. The patient is a long-standing diabetic and notes that the symptoms have been progressing over the last several months. The patient has been taking over the counter and prescription medication for indigestion and esophageal reflux without relief. Upon examination, the patient complains of mild tenderness in the epigastric area and right upper quadrant. A gastric motility study is planned in conjunction with an upper GI endoscopy.

## What Documentation Is Required to Support the Services Provided?

The physician must first identify the most generally accepted content of the interpretation and report. The written entry should answer the following questions:

**Why is the test being performed?** Give the questionable symptoms or the medical condition being followed in an easily identifiable location. In the above scenario, the interpretation and report of both the upper GI and the motility study should indicate that both tests are being performed to determine the source of the patient's complaints. The conditions, signs and symptoms also should be identified in the order for the test.

**What was found; were the results as expected or were there new findings?** The interpretation of the upper GI should indicate the findings from the study, such as the presence or absence of lesions, erythema, etc. The interpretation of the motility study should document the functioning of the esophagus and stomach, including pressure measurements as well as any other anomalies.

**Finally, how do the results affect the treatment of the patient's medical condition?** Both tests must indicate or support the need for further tests or specific medical treatment.

The results of the test should be recorded by the interpreting physician in a conspicuous area of the chart, on the actual printout, or in a separate interpretation and report. If the test is a photo that is stored on film or in a computer, the location of the photo must be clearly noted in the chart. Finally, these test results must be easily retrievable in the event of an audit.

With respect to billing for the performance of a diagnostic test, if the physician has confirmed his diagnosis based upon the results of the test, the physician may use that ICD-9 code, with the signs and symptoms that prompted the test as additional diagnoses. If the test is normal, the claim should be submitted using the patient's initial signs and symptoms. When a diagnostic test is ordered in the absence of signs, symptoms, or other evidence of illness, however, then the ICD-9 code should reflect that the test was done for screening purposes. The results of the test, if any, may be reported as additional diagnoses.

After attending a conference on fraud and abuse risk areas for gastroenterologists, the physicians of Digestive Disease Associates ("DDA") agree to implement a compliance program to ensure all DDA patients receive high-quality, medically necessary, and appropriately billed professional services in compliance with all legal, regulatory, and ethical requirements. In order to identify potential billing and coding risks for DDA, DDA's compliance attorney hires a consultant to audit a sample of DDA's medical and billing records. The consultant reports that of the 30 E/M services he reviewed, he disagreed with the level of code selected by the DDA physicians in 18 instances. According to the consultant, the documentation in the medical record did not support the level 4 or 5 E/M code selected in each instance. When the attorney and consultant meet with the DDA medical staff to discuss the documentation insufficiencies and methods to improve in this area, the physicians disagree with the consultant's findings, stating that regardless of the information found in the medical records, their patients are very complicated, and, therefore, meet the CPT code requirements.

## WHAT INFORMATION MUST A MEDICAL RECORD INCLUDE TO SUPPORT CLAIMS FOR E/M SERVICES?

The issue of proper coding is extremely complex, particularly in the area of E/M coding related to new and established patients. The CPT descriptor of the service represented by a particular code establishes the various components of care a physician must perform and document in order to bill for a particular service. Nevertheless, the medical community and government have long recognized the difficulties with the E/M codes and documentation parameters used to justify billing a particular level code. In response, the CMS developed documentation guidelines (DGs) to supplement the CPT code descriptors. These guidelines specify what information must be in a patient's medical record in order to support billing at the various E/M levels.

The first DGs went into effect in September 1995 (1995 DGs) for use by carriers in performing medical review of E/M codes. The 1995 DGs drew immediate criticism because the documentation required to bill for a single system examination was not clear. It was felt that medical reviewers did not give credit for complete single system physical examinations, and, therefore, it was impossible for specialists to meet the higher documentation requirements for the higher level E/M services. In response to this opposition to the 1995 DGs, CMS developed a new set of guidelines (1997 DGs) with assistance from the AMA that were intended to be more appropriate for single system examinations and to revise and clarify some of the information in the 1995 DGs.

The 1997 DGs require physicians to document a certain number of elements of a physical examination and assign numerical values to entries in the medical record. The level of E/M service is in turn intended to correlate to the "documentation score." The 1997 DGs were expected to replace the 1995 DGs; like the earlier version, however, physicians opposed the new guidelines on the basis that they were too complicated, too time-consuming, and placed too much emphasis on documentation. In light of this opposition, CMS instructed carriers to use either the 1995 and 1997 DGs when reviewing medical records, and committed to develop yet a third version of DGs. The third version, issued in draft in 1999, incorporated a multitude of clinical vignettes to help guide physicians' E/M code selections, but once again, the DGs were criticized as creating a system that is too difficult to follow and could result in inconsistent review of providers.

To date, the 1999 DGs have not been finalized, and the Secretary of the Department of Health and Human Services testified before Congress that the clinical vignette project would be discontinued. Consequently, the 1995 and 1997 DGs stand as the relevant documentation guidance for physicians and other health care providers who submit claims for E/M services. While the DDA physicians may believe that the services rendered to their patients are consistent with certain E/M code descriptors, if the documentation in the relevant patient's medical record does not meet the documentation requirements outlined in either the 1995 or 1997 guidelines, the DDA physicians are at significant risk for having payment for their services denied. Furthermore, DDA could face allegations of submitting false claims to the government if the physicians knowingly continue to submit claims for a level of service to Medicare beneficiaries that is not reflected in the medical record. Without proper documentation, it is nearly impossible to prove that a service reflected on a claim form was the service actually received by the patient.

Dr. Smith hires an advertising agency to assist in promoting his GI practice. The advertising agency develops a comprehensive ad campaign and presents it to Dr. Smith for his review and approval. The advertising promotes the physician as being "one of the best gastroenterologists in the area," a colonoscopy as "painless," and "guarantees that the procedure will accurately establish your risk for cancer." In addition, the ad contains a quote from one of the practice's happy patients saying, "Thanks to Dr. Smith, I now have the peace of mind of knowing that I don't have colon cancer."

## Is the Ad Copy Acceptable?

The advertisement described above contains a number of serious problems. The Federal Trade Commission (FTC), as well as several state medical boards, have taken action against physicians whose advertising is considered to be false or misleading. Any advertising to the public must be truthful, and all facts stated must be capable of being substantiated. Further, any description of results must reflect the results of the typical patient. Some states have even more restrictive provisions, such as a prohibition on claims of superiority or the use of patient testimonials.

With respect to the advertisement in question, while it may be a true statement that the physician is one of the best gastroenterologists in the area, that is a claim that is very hard to substantiate. Furthermore, in a state that prohibits claims of superiority, even if the statement could be substantiated, it may be prohibited. The suggestion that a procedure is "painless" always raises a red flag. The use of anesthetic or the need to prescribe even over the counter painkillers postprocedure is an acknowledgment that the procedure is not painless. "Painless" is a word to avoid in any marketing. The word "guarantee" is also problematic, as there is no assurance that this will be true in every case. Finally, the use of the patient testimonial without some type of qualifier that results may vary from patient to patient also is likely to be a problem. As indicated previously, some states prohibit the use of any patient testimonials. While the constitutionality of such prohibition is subject to challenge, any such challenge will be expensive and time-consuming; if a physician is in a state that prohibits patient testimonials, he or she should consider the potential risk carefully before using them in marketing.

# PHARMACEUTICAL COMPANY RELATIONSHIPS

A pharmaceutical company (the "Company") has a breakthrough product that has just been approved for Medicare reimbursement. Dr. Smith was one of the drug's clinical investigators, and believes that the drug is a significant advancement that will greatly benefit patients with duodenal ulcers worldwide. Dr. Smith is well known and very well respected in his specialty. He is approached by the Company to give a presentation sharing his experience as an investigator relating to the product at a worldwide gastroenterology conference in Paris, France. The Company offers to pay for Dr. Smith's expenses, including first-class airfare from his home in Chicago, meals, a week's stay at a hotel in Paris, plus an honorarium of $10,000. The Company is careful not to interfere in any way with the content or conclusion of Dr. Smith's presentation.

## MAY DR. SMITH ACCEPT THE COMPANY'S OFFER?

Relationships between physicians and pharmaceutical companies are targets for examination and enforcement by government authorities. Important recent developments in this area include the TAP Pharmaceuticals investigation and settlement, the HHS Office of Inspector General's (OIG) FY 2002 Work Plan, and the *Compliance Program Guidance for Pharmaceutical Manufacturers.* Physicians also should be aware of the renewed government awareness of the AMA's *Ethical Guidelines on Gifts to Physicians from Industry* and the similar guidelines from PhRMA, the national trade association of major brand name pharmaceutical manufacturers.

The OIG work plan indicates that the OIG plans to enlarge its focus on the relationships between physicians and pharmaceutical companies. The OIG is concerned about such companies providing anything of value to physicians and other health care providers as an inducement to order company products. In the view of the OIG, such conduct creates both inherent conflicts of interest as well as potential violations of the Federal Anti-Kickback Statute. The Federal Anti-Kickback Statute prohibits the knowing offer or receipt of anything of value in exchange for referring, recommending, or arranging for a product or service paid for by a federal health care program.

Not all physician relationships with pharmaceutical companies are prohibited or inappropriate, however. To avoid unreasonable risks, several basic principles should be followed. For example, with respect to receipt of anything of value in return for presenting at conferences, individuals who are bona fide meeting faculty, company consultants, or researchers may receive *reasonable compensation for services rendered*. These services should be provided pursuant to an appropriate written contract. It also is appropriate for compensation from pharmaceutical companies for such personal services to include reasonable travel costs and either an honorarium or payment for the faculty member's time. Payment should reflect fair market value for the physician's time, recognizing that the time involved includes preparation of the presentation and travel away from one's practice, in addition to the actual presentation itself. If a physician believes that the benefits received exceed the value of the contribution made, the physician should consider a reevaluation of the relationship. Further, physicians should at all times retain responsibility and control over the content of their lecture.

Applying these principles, the above example raises issues for Dr. Smith as well as the Company. Even assuming that Dr. Smith's presentation and the conference itself would be of bona fide value, with the content solely under his control, the arrangement must reflect reasonable fair market value payment for services provided. The Paris location, the first-class airline ticket and the four star hotel all serve to heighten the scrutiny of enforcement officials. These alone, however, are unlikely to trigger any accusation that the kickback law has been violated. Two aspects of the arrangement, however, may raise questions.

First, coverage of 1 week at a four star hotel when Dr. Smith appears to be making a single 45-minute presentation may raise questions, particularly if Dr. Smith's spouse accompanied Dr. Smith to Paris, and the couple spent the remainder of the week sightseeing. On the other hand, if Dr. Smith remains at the conference and continues to confer with other physicians about the new drug, the weeklong stay could be appropriate.

Similarly, the $10,000 honorarium appears high for a 45-minute presentation but, again, this presumably covers preparation time, as well as lost time away from Dr. Smith's practice. The key to defending the propriety of the honorarium is to be able to document the time spent by Dr. Smith on behalf of the Company, and to demonstrate that the honorarium reflects fair market value for that time.

# PROFESSIONAL COURTESY DISCOUNTS

Quality Gastroenterology, P.C. ("PC") extends professional courtesy discounts to internists and general practitioners who are in active practice within a 50-mile radius of PC as well the families of these providers. PC's professional courtesy policy consists of waiving any coinsurance obligation these individuals may be required to pay to Medicare or any private third-party payer (ie, "insurance-only" billing). Some, but not all, of the recipients of PC's professional courtesy policy refer patients to PC.

## DOES PC'S PROFESSIONAL COURTESY POLICY PLACE THE PRACTICE AT RISK?

Professional courtesy may raise fraud and abuse concerns, particularly where recipients of professional courtesy are selected in a manner that directly or indirectly takes into account their ability to affect referrals or otherwise generate business for the physician offering the free or discounted service. Where Medicare services are involved, both the Federal Anti-Kickback Statute and the Patient Inducement Prohibition may be implicated. If the professional courtesy extends to services paid for by commercial insurers, state anti-kickback and insurance fraud laws may be triggered.

In its *Compliance Program Guidance for Individual and Small Group Physician Practices*, the OIG set forth guidance regarding professional courtesy discounts. According to the OIG, a physician's risk of violating the Federal Anti-Kickback Statute is reduced significantly where a physician has a regular and consistent policy of extending professional courtesy to both referral and nonreferral sources and in a manner that does not take ability to refer into account. In fact, the OIG stated that physicians who regularly waive the entire fee for services or coinsurance amounts to a group of persons might not implicate the fraud and abuse laws, so long as membership in the group receiving the courtesy is not based on a person's ability to refer patients to the physician either directly or indirectly. The legality of any professional courtesy arrangement, however, will turn on the specific facts presented, and in respect to allegations that a physician violated the Federal Anti-Kickback Statute, on the specific intent of the parties involved.

Aside from the issue of whether the Federal Anti-Kickback Statute is triggered, the OIG was clear in the *Compliance Program Guidance*, and again in a 2001 Advisory Opinion, that, except in circumstances of documented patient financial hardship, any waiver of a Medicare fee-for-service copayment by a physician practice is viewed as an improper patient inducement because it is likely to influence a beneficiary's decision as to where to receive services. This would be considered a violation of the Patient Inducement Prohibition and subject the physician practice to civil money penalties.

PC's professional courtesy policy raises some concern and should be modified. The government could allege that by extending professional courtesy only to those internists and general practitioners in active practice and located within a 50-mile radius of PC, the policy is designed to limit professional courtesy to those who are likely to be referral sources. The policy instead should eliminate any geographic restrictions, and should apply equally to all physicians regardless of whether they are in active practice or retired. Furthermore, PC's policy of insurance-only billing runs the risk that it may run afoul of the state insurance fraud laws and patient inducement prohibitions. PC could eliminate this risk by implementing a policy to waive the entire fee rather than just any requisite copayments. Insurance-only billing should be limited to patient financial, not courtesy, considerations.

# 23

## Using Medicare Utilization Data to Identify Potential Coding Issues

At least once a year, Medicare profiles each physician who submits a Medicare claim. One physician in a large gastroenterology practice recently was selected by its Medicare carrier for a comprehensive medical review due to a significant variance between the gastroenterologist's coding patterns for evaluation and management services and that of his peers. The physician and the practice wonder how they could have prevented being subject to such an audit.

### A Proactive Approach

Utilization profiles are used by Medicare carriers to identify potential coding problems. The more frequently a physician bills a particular service, the more likely the physician will be subject to a postpayment audit. Specialty physicians are compared to their peers, although such information is not foolproof. Practice patterns vary throughout the United States and there may be special circumstances that support extraordinary utilization rates.

Instead of waiting for "the letter" requesting records, the practice could have taken a proactive approach to determine if an audit issue existed within the office. Medicare data is available commercially to help providers compare their practice patterns with national norms. Additionally, Medicare has made provider utilization data available on request. Significant deviations may indicate potential concerns.

Consider this example of established patient office visits.

| CPT Code | Provider Peer | Group |
|----------|---------------|-------|
| 99211 | 0.82% | 2.63% |
| 99212 | 1.29% | 16.29% |
| 99213 | 4.56% | 53.58% |
| 99214 | 93.19% | 23.76% |
| 99215 | 0.14% | 3.74% |

In this example, a potential overutilization issue exists with CPT code 99214, as it appears that nearly all established patient office visits are billed at this level. From a Medicare standpoint, an auditor would be curious to know if the physician's documentation for 99214 claims supports the specific elements of detailed history and examination, and medical decision-making of moderate complexity. In addition, the auditor would be interested in knowing if special circumstances existed that would justify the extraordinary rate of these claims. It is foreseeable that an auditor would doubt whether 93% of all established patients presented with a worsening problem or new condition that warranted such a comprehensive level of service.

## What to Do

Once the practice discovered such a significant discrepancy, it should have requested a chart audit by an impartial and qualified person. Depending upon the extent of the variation, the practice might consider conducting the audit under attorney-client privilege for the protection of the physician and the practice. Education on appropriate coding and documentation should be conducted with each gastroenterologist, particularly if the audit identified problems. Finally, the practice should conduct annual utilization analyses and audits to ensure continued compliance.

# 24

A gastroenterologist practice receives a scheduling call from a internist's office (Dr. Anderson) from which the GI group often receives referrals. The staff person from Dr. Anderson's office asks that the gastroenterologist (Dr. Miller) "see and evaluate the patient for Dr. Anderson." The patient is a Medicare patient. The chief complaint is filled out: "Patient referred by Dr. Anderson for consultation."

The patient comes to the office and is evaluated. Dr. Miller orders diagnostic tests and follow-up services, as indicated by the examination. After the visit, Dr. Miller sends a consultation letter to Dr. Anderson. Dr. Miller's office bills the Medicare program for a consultation.

## IS THIS A CONSULTATION?

Was Dr. Miller's evaluation of the patient a consultation, as that term is defined by the Medicare program?

According to the Medicare program, a consultation is provided by a physician whose opinion or advice regarding the evaluation or management of a specific problem is requested by another physician or appropriate practitioner. In other words, the hallmark of a consultation is *the subjective intent of the requesting physician to receive advice or an opinion*. The request for the consultation and the need for the consultation must be documented in the patient's medical record. Further, the consultant must prepare a written report of his or her findings, and the report must be provided to the requesting physician or practitioner.

The Medicare program will not consider the session to be a consultation if there has been a *transfer of care*. A transfer of care occurs when the referring physician transfers the responsibility for the patient's complete care for the relevant problem or issue, at the time of the referral.

Applied to the situation above, many of the consultation requirements appear to be met. However, the crucial element here, as is so often the case, is the intent of the requesting physician. Again, Medicare rules require that the initial physician *requests* the consultation.

In the hypothetical, the initiation came verbally from Dr. Anderson's office, and asked for an *evaluation*. How do we know what the initiating physician was requesting? Was it a consultation or was it simply a request for an evaluation and management or a GI service?

Dr. Anderson's request was, unfortunately, ambiguous. Although Dr. Anderson's request for a review might be interpreted to suggest that a consultation was desired, the failure of the requesting physician's office to specifically request a *consultation*, and Dr. Miller's scheduler's failure to clarify the nature of the request, make the classification of this service ultimately a matter of guesswork. The chief complaint entry, despite the fact that it uses the word *consultation*, actually complicates the problem by using the term *referral*. In Medicare parlance, there is no *referral or referring physician* in a consultation service. Those terms are considered to be consistent only with situations where the care of the patient is transferred from the initiating physician or practitioner to another provider of care.

# 25

# SCREENING VS DIAGNOSTIC COLONOSCOPY

For Medicare billing purposes, a *screening* colonoscopy is a procedure performed on a patient who presents free of any signs or symptoms whatsoever and for whom no significant findings are noted during the procedure. While the patient may be at "high risk" to the extent that he or she may be within the age group for which cancer screening is recommended; has a prior, but now resolved condition that is in some way associated with colon cancer; or has a family history of colon disease, a screening procedure should be billed absent current signs or symptoms or unless the findings of the procedure justify billing as a diagnostic colonoscopy. The appropriate Medicare billing codes are G0121 for the average risk patient and G0105 for the high-risk patient. The supporting ICD-9 code for screening colonoscopies on average-risk patients is V76.51 (special screenings for malignant neoplasm of the colon) and includes V16.01, among others, for high-risk patients (family history of malignant neoplasm of the gastrointestinal tract).

By comparison, a *diagnostic* colonoscopy is a procedure performed on a person who either presents with signs or symptoms of colon disease or for whom a malignant neoplasm or other abnormal or premalignant condition of the colon is discovered during the course of the procedure, even if no signs or symptoms were present prior to beginning the procedure. For billing, the 45378 CPT code is used along with appropriate ICD-9 code for the findings.

# 26

## DOCUMENTATION REQUIREMENTS BEYOND MEDICARE

A 38-year-old woman presents with complaints of chronic diarrhea accompanied by abdominal pain, which she has experienced for about 3 months. She reports no sense of bloating or fullness, but has noticed that her belly becomes gradually larger during the course of the day, and is always back to normal size each morning. Her primary care physician ordered routine blood and stool tests, which were negative, prior to referring her to the gastroenterologist.

The specialist ascertains that the patient has two children and currently uses an oral contraceptive. When asked about diet, the patient states that she has followed a lactose elimination diet for 4 weeks and has noticed no change in her symptoms. As the patient already has a medical record at the practice, in connection with an appendectomy 9 years earlier, the physician notes the history of the current condition briefly: "Chronic diarr, rec onset—IBS? CBC stool neg." He then orders an abdominal ultrasound for the patient.

The office manager reviews the order before arranging the referral and calls the gastroenterologist to ask for specific findings to support a request for an ultrasound, as opposed to an endoscopy or small bowel series. The physician replies, "This isn't Medicare, so I don't have to follow all those guidelines."

## DO THE DOCUMENTATION GUIDELINES EXTEND BEYOND MEDICARE?

The basic principles of chart documentation extend beyond Medicare and apply to all types of medical and surgical services. They include:

- The medical record should be complete and legible.

- Notes for each encounter should include:
  - date of service
  - subjective complaint
  - history relevant to the complaint
  - exam findings
  - assessment
  - plan
  - legible provider signature

The appropriateness of a particular procedure is judged on the basis of the documentation of these basic elements. Professionalism requires a complete record of patient services, regardless of the requirements imposed by particular payers.

Diagnosis in cases of diarrhea or abdominal pain is notoriously challenging because of the numerous potential causes and the tendency of one condition to mimic another. In the case of this patient, where the signs appear to point to irritable bowel syndrome (IBS), the more common choices would be endoscopy or x-ray (which sometimes, although not always, can confirm IBS) instead of ultrasound (which has no proven utility for diagnosing IBS). To support his sonography order, the doctor must expand his cursory history to include reference to the woman's risk factors for gallstones (ie, the hormonal factors of having experienced pregnancy and currently using oral contraceptives), which can be present before separate symptoms emerge and are readily identified through ultrasound. A health plan gatekeeper would be likely to object to the more costly procedure in the absence of a rational basis—and would be highly unlikely to "fill in the blanks" with inferences that clinicians may consider obvious.

Documentation guidelines extend beyond Medicare, and any payer can impose postpayment review. Furthermore, the importance of thorough documentation has significance beyond reimbursement concerns. The medical record is a tool for planning and assessing the patient's treatment and sharing treatment information with other medical professionals, and might even furnish data for research on modalities and outcomes.

# DIAGNOSIS CODING

In an effort to consolidate their billing functions, a large group practice with several satellite locations centralized its billing office at one location. The route slips (or superbills) were completed by the physicians and staff and couriered to the billing office for data entry and claim submission. The billing office staff relied on the route slips to bill the service provided, the level of service, and appropriate diagnosis codes. Many of the route slips contained three or more diagnosis codes. The billing staff mechanically listed all the diagnosis codes on the claims.

## HOW DOES DIAGNOSIS CODING INFLUENCE REIMBURSEMENT?

The proper use of diagnosis codes (ICD-9) serves as the mechanism to advise a payer of the reason a particular procedure or service was performed. Use of an improper ICD-9 code can result in a payment for a service that is not covered, or denial of a payment for a service that should be covered.

Several considerations should be made when an ICD-9 code is selected for the claim form.

- Be as specific as possible and consistent with the patient's medical record. The most specific ICD-9 codes have four or five digits. Using nonspecific codes may not reveal adequate medical necessity for the service.
- A history of the disease may be appropriate for a condition that no longer exists (ie, V-codes).
- Code symptoms if no definitive diagnosis can be determined. Do not describe the patient with a disease or condition he/she does not have. "Rule out" does not exist in the ICD-9 manual.

- Document whether the condition is chronic or acute and the planned treatment. If it is acute in an emergency situation, be sure to identify the nature of the condition. A chronic disease can be listed multiple times as long as it continues to be treated.
- Identify how injuries occurred.
- List chronic conditions or secondary diagnoses only if they are pertinent to that particular visit.
- Be consistent with CPT rules. For example, if you use a separate procedure code, then identify an additional diagnosis to justify that service.
- Understand the third-party payer guidelines. Some payers truncate the diagnosis list and ignore the second or third ICD-9 code.

The critical problem in this case is the failure of the biller to be able to determine the precise diagnosis code that reflected the physician's decision to provide a procedure or service. Further, the physicians continued to include diagnoses based on the patient's prior ocular history. This further confused the billers. Where physicians use billers either within their practice or contract out for such services, they must take care to ensure that the services performed and the reason for the services are clearly identified and linked on the route slip.

# CLINICAL RESEARCH COVERAGE UNDER MEDICARE

A 68-year-old patient with severe ulcerative colitis has not responded to corticosteroid therapy. His gastroenterologist reads that a study of an investigational injection drug for steroid-refractory ulcerative colitis is currently recruiting. In order to verify his condition, however, the patient will need a new diagnostic test, because his colonoscopy occurred more than 3 years ago. "No problem," says the physician. "Medicare is paying for care in clinical trials now, so we'll just scope you again and get you in!" A few weeks later, the gastroenterologist finds a denial from her Medicare carrier on her desk.

## WHAT WENT WRONG?

To begin with, a diagnostic test performed solely for the purpose of establishing a beneficiary's eligibility for a clinical trial is not covered. Even if she had performed a medically necessary service within the scope of Medicare clinical trial coverage, she would not be entitled to payment if the trial, by its terms, furnished free medical care to participants. Also, she has no idea whether the trial has federal sponsorship or otherwise qualifies, in terms of purpose, design, scientific validity, and various ethical standards, for Medicare coverage.

Medicare, along with other payers, is offering more help to gastroenterology patients at both ends of the spectrum: beneficiaries have access to screening examinations to catch early signs of disease, and they are also able to use their Medicare benefit to defray the costs of participating in certain clinical trials for conditions that have not responded to treatment. However, before billing for services to a beneficiary participating in a clinical trial, it is important to know which trials, and which services, qualify for Medicare payment.

A qualifying trial must:

- Study an item or service that falls within a Medicare benefit category (eg, a physician's service or a diagnostic test) and that is not subject to a statutory exclusion (eg, hearing aids).
- Have a therapeutic intent.
- Enroll diagnosed beneficiaries (exclusively if the trial is of a therapeutic intervention, or along with healthy controls if trial is of a diagnostic intervention).
- Have "desirable characteristics," ie, have valid scientific support, avoid duplicating existing studies, be well-designed to answer the question posed by the research, comply with federal standards for scientific integrity and protection of human research subjects. A trial is deemed to have desirable characteristics if it is one of the following:
    - funded by certain federal agencies (eg, NIH, CDC, DOD)
    - supported by centers of cooperative groups sponsored by those agencies
    - conducted under an FDA investigational new drug application (IND)
    - IND-exempt

Routine (covered) costs of clinical trials include items and services that would be: (1) considered medically necessary in the absence of a clinical trial, (2) required for the provision of the investigational item or service, (3) clinically appropriate for monitoring the effects of the investigational item or service or for preventing complications, and (4) medically necessary to diagnose and treat complications that arise from the investigational item or service.

Noncovered costs would typically include those associated with items or services that: (1) have no Medicare benefit category, (2) are excluded from coverage by statute or national noncoverage policy, (3) are used for data collection and analysis rather than clinical management of the patient (ie, monthly CT scans for a condition that usually requires a single scan), (4) are furnished at no charge by research sponsors, and (5) are provided solely to determine whether the patient is eligible for the trial.

## MEDICAL NECESSITY

A Medicare patient with a family history of pancreatic cancer presents with complaints of persistent heartburn that has not responded to changes in diet and use of daily over the counter H2 antagonists. The patient also reports occasional difficulty in swallowing. The physician performs an upper gastrointestinal endoscopy with ultrasound.

### DID THE PATIENT'S CONDITION QUALIFY FOR UPPER ENDOSCOPY WITH ULTRASOUND?

No, the patient's symptoms suggest a diagnosis supporting upper gastrointestinal endoscopy only. The physician's reason for performing the ultrasound was not a symptom or finding suggesting the presence of pancreatic disease, but rather the patient's family history of cancer of the pancreas, and in this case the ultrasound was a (noncovered) screening procedure. Accordingly, Medicare should have been billed only for the upper gastrointestinal endoscopy, which would have sufficed to identify or rule out the possible causes of his symptoms.

Medicare carriers' Local Medical Review Policies offer specific guidance as to the diagnoses and findings that support the need for diagnostic services. Physicians should review updates from their carriers for changes to these policies, especially with respect to relatively new technologies. Also, it is important that a physician record in the medical record all diagnoses and findings that influence her choice of a particular procedure, to enable billing personnel to make use of new diagnostic codes as they are added to identify specialized conditions and risk factors.

## Billing for Services Rendered by a Physician Subcontractor

A gastroenterology practice contracts with a liver specialist to provide services to its patients. The agreement with the specialist is on a part-time basis and classifies the specialist as an independent contractor. The practice bills for and receives payment for the office-based services provided by the specialist. The practice also bills for and receives payment for any surgical procedures provided to the practice's patients by the specialist at a nearby ambulatory surgery center. The ambulatory surgery center is owned by the practice's surgeons as well as other nongastroenterology surgeons. The liver specialist is paid 30% of the net collections attributable to the services he performs.

### May the Practice Bill for and Compensate a Physician Independent Contractor Based on a Percentage of Revenue Generated by the Physician?

The proposed arrangement is not in compliance with the Medicare reassignment rules. Those rules generally prohibit anyone other than the person who actually provides a service from collecting the payment for the service. There are exceptions to the reassignment prohibition, the most relevant of which allows a practice to bill for services rendered by an independent contractor as long as those services are provided in premises owned or leased by the practice. While this would allow the practice to bill for the office-based services rendered by the specialist, since the ASC is not an asset or a wholly owned subsidiary of the practice, the practice could not bill for the surgery performed by the specialist at the ASC.

This arrangement also raises issues under the Federal Anti-Kickback Statute as well as the anti-kickback statute in states that have similar prohibitions. That statute makes it a violation of both criminal and civil law for any person knowingly and willfully to pay anything, directly or indirectly, in cash or in kind, to reward or induce a referral for any service covered by a federally funded health care program. Safe harbor regulations promulgated by the OIG provide protection for certain personal services arrangements. To qualify for the safe harbor, however, payment must be fixed, set in advance, and not vary with the value or volume of referrals.

An arrangement need not comply with a safe harbor to avoid violating the statute, however. In situations where a safe harbor does not apply, the government is likely to focus on the question of whether a relationship reflects fair market value. Where it does not, the concern is that there may be an intent to reward or induce referrals. Here, the government might question whether 30% reflects fair market value for the liver specialist's services, or, perhaps more appropriately, since the practice is the source of referrals for the specialist, whether the practice's retention of 70% of revenue is reasonable to cover the overhead of the practice. The analysis of the appropriateness of the arrangement must include consideration of the fact that, with respect to surgical services, most of the related overhead is being borne by the ambulatory surgery center, not the practice.

In addition to the issues discussed above, the arrangement could raise concerns under state fee-splitting prohibitions. Although some state medical boards are not inclined to challenge the propriety of percentage-based compensation arrangements when such arrangements occur within physician group practices, other boards find these kinds of terms to be inappropriate, even within the context of a group practice.

Aside from restructuring the arrangement to comply with the reassignment rules and to avoid the anti-kickback and fee splitting risks, there is one alternative consideration. Both the reassignment rules as well as the anti-kickback statutes have exceptions for bona fide employees. Similarly, state fee splitting prohibitions generally do not apply to employees of a physician practice. Therefore, if the parties were willing, the liver specialist might be able to become an employee of the practice under the same financial terms as outlined above.

Dr. Beck, an internist, has a standing order in his practice that he recommends all patients over 50 years of age to undergo screening for colorectal cancer. Mr. Matthews, a 56-year-old man, visits Dr. Beck for his annual physical examination. Aside from severe secondary glaucoma, Mr. Matthews is otherwise in good health. Upon review of Mr. Matthews' chart, Dr. Beck realizes that he has never been screened for colorectal cancer. Dr. Beck refers Mr. Matthews to Dr. Thompson, head of gastroenterology at the local hospital. Dr. Thompson examines Mr. Matthews and orders a screening colonoscopy even though there are no symptoms or family history of any colorectal disease. Mr. Matthews receives Social Security Disability Benefits and coverage under Medicare due to loss of vision.

## ARE THERE ANY GUIDELINES TO LET US KNOW WHEN A PROCEDURE TO SCREEN FOR COLORECTAL CANCER MAY BE BILLED?

### Fecal Occult Blood Test

Medicare covers a screening FOBT annually for a patient who is age 50 or older and is entitled to Medicare Part B benefits. Many insurance plans also cover a screening FOBT once a year starting at age 50.

### Flexible Sigmoidoscopy

Medicare covers a screening Flex Sig once every 4 years for a patient who is 50 years of age or older and is entitled to Medicare Part B benefits. Screening Flex Sig may be billed when the patient has an absence of signs or symptoms that would be an indication for sigmoidoscopy or colonoscopy. Typically, the various Medicare carriers require a screening diagnosis code. Many insurance plans also cover a screening Flex Sig once every 4 to 5 years beginning at age 50.

## Colonoscopy

Medicare will approve a screening colonoscopy for a patient at *high* risk once every 2 years if the patient is 50 years of age or older and is entitled to Medicare Part B benefits. High-risk patients include:

- A close relative (sibling, parent or child) who has had colorectal cancer or an adenomatous polyp.
- A family history of familial adenomatous polyposis.
- A family history of hereditary nonpolyposis colorectal cancer.
- A personal history of adenomatous polyps.
- A personal history of colorectal cancer.
- Inflammatory bowel disease, including Crohn's disease or ulcerative colitis.

Medicare will approve a screening colonoscopy for a patient at *average* risk once every 10 years for a patient who is 50 years of age or older and is entitled to Medicare Part B benefits. A screening colonoscopy for a patient at average risk will be denied if the patient has had a screening Flex Sig within the previous 4 years.

In the above scenario, Mr. Matthews would be classified as an average risk patient and would receive coverage for the screening colonoscopy under Medicare. However, unless an event occurs to bring Mr. Matthews into the high-risk category, Medicare will not cover another colonoscopy performed within less than 10 years from the date of Mr. Matthew's first screening colonoscopy.

Coverage by many insurance plans for screening colonoscopies is variable. Screening colonoscopies are generally considered warranted once every 10 years starting at age 50 for people with no family or personal history of polyps and no symptoms of any illness. Most plans will cover a colonoscopy if it is needed for a follow-up test or diagnosing a problem.

# DOCUMENTATION IN THE ELECTRONIC AGE

Most physicians know by now that they have to have a system for tracking telephone conversations so that new developments, and any treatment decisions they inspire, end up in the patient's chart. But how are you accounting for electronic mail correspondence with your patients? It is much easier to exchange information and solve problems now that a "real-time" conversation isn't required, but e-mail brings its own complications.

Ask yourself:

- Are you promptly transferring e-mail exchanges to the medical record? If not, are you using some form of back-up so that the messages won't be lost in cyberspace before they are charted?
- Do you use an encryption program to protect the confidentiality of the identifiable patient information?
- Have you told your patients what kinds of messages should and should not be sent electronically? Do they know how your mail is retrieved when you are out of town, or how long it will go unanswered if there is no retrieval process?

For all kinds of electronic records, the issue of back-up is a serious consideration. State law establishes retention periods for medical records, and these obligations are violated whether someone throws away paper records too soon or loses data by spilling coffee on a workstation. Also, as with electronic mail, there are threats to the security of electronic records that may require solutions more sophisticated than locked file drawers, and include "firewall" programs, regular password changes, and up-to-date virus protections. Unauthorized access to patient records can create multiple liabilities with respect to state and federal civil remedies and criminal sanctions, private actions on the part of patients, and disqualification for payment by Medicare and other programs.

# LEGAL ISSUES

A patient arrives 15 minutes late for her appointment at her physician's office for an office-based procedure. Upon checking in with the receptionist, the patient is handed several informed consent forms and is told to "hurry up and fill these out". The patient is told that if she has any questions, a nurse is available to answer or assist. The receptionist instructs the patient to take a seat in the waiting area. The patient signs the forms, returns them to the receptionist and does not ask to speak with a nurse.

## HAS THE PATIENT GIVEN INFORMED CONSENT?

Many physicians believe that as long as a patient has signed the informed consent form, the physician has fulfilled the "informed consent" requirement and that he or she is protected. A signed piece of paper, however, is not a guarantee of informed consent. Rather, "informed consent" is a process designed to ensure that a patient understands the risks and benefits of various medical procedures as well as the alternatives to that treatment, and, absent physician negligence, to protect physicians from liability for those risks that the patient assumes. Although a signed informed consent form is strong evidence of the patient's awareness, it is not uncommon for courts to look past the document itself and determine if true "informed consent" took place. A complete informed consent process should: (1) describe the procedure for which the patient is being asked to give consent, (2) discuss the attendant risks and benefits, (3) notify the patient of alternative courses of treatment in a way in which the patient understands the information, (4) provide the patient with sufficient time to process the information, and (5) provide meaningful opportunity for questions.

There are several informed consent issues raised in the described scenario. First, patients must be given sufficient time to digest the information that has been provided to them. In the above scenario, although it is not the physician's fault that the patient arrived late for her appointment, a rushed signature on a consent form is unlikely to provide time for the patient to read and understand the information.

Second, patients should be given a meaningful opportunity to ask questions of their physician about the information presented. In the described scenario, the patient clearly did not have a meaningful opportunity to ask questions. In part this was due to the rushed nature of this particular encounter. Even under these circumstances, however, when the patient was taken to the office for the procedure, a nurse should have reviewed the informed consent form with the patient, making certain that the patient had, in fact, reviewed and understood it, and encouraged the patient to ask questions if necessary.

Finally, beyond having a nurse review the form with the patient, ultimately it is the physician who performs the procedure, and who is responsible for obtaining a patient's informed consent. It is the operating physician's duty as well as in his or her best interest to ensure a patient has made an informed decision as to whether to submit to a proposed procedure. The best way for a physician to ensure and be confident that the patient understands the information is to participate personally in the process and be available for questions.

A physician is treating a patient for ulcerative colitis. The patient has been unresponsive to traditional drug treatment, and the physician recommends moving to a new therapy, infliximab. While infliximab is an FDA approved drug, the treatment of ulcerative colitis is not one of its approved indications. The physician has been reading, however, about the positive clinical trial results. In discussions between the physician and patient about the proposed new therapy, the patient is not advised of the off-label use of the drug.

## DOES OFF-LABEL USE REQUIRE
## A DIFFERENT INFORMED CONSENT?

There is no legal restriction against a physician using an FDA-approved pharmaceutical product for an off-label use. Physicians are recognized as having the right to exercise their professional medical judgment within the scope of their practice. Because such off-label use has become commonplace, in such cases patients frequently are given no additional information about off-label use. From a risk management perspective, however, it is always safer to ensure that the patient is fully informed about all of the elements involved in a particular recommended treatment, including the fact that the physician intends to recommend an unapproved use.

This issue is one that is rarely tested. The adequacy of the informed consent becomes an issue only in the context of malpractice litigation. If there is a bad result, however, a plaintiff's attorney will almost certainly focus on the adequacy of the informed consent. Failure to include information relating to off-label use will be an attractive argument to make to the jury. It is an argument that can be minimized significantly if the patient has received the information as part of the informed consent process.

# REFUND OF OVERPAYMENTS

During a routine self-audit, the compliance officer for Gastroenterology Practice ("the Practice") discovered that the Practice had been submitting claims for a particular service using the incorrect CPT code. An internal investigation by the billing supervisor revealed that the error was due to a misunderstanding among the staff and that as a result the Practice was paid more than it should have been for the service at issue.

## WHAT IS THE PRACTICE'S RESPONSIBILITY TO THE MEDICARE PROGRAM WHEN IT DISCOVERS IT HAS BEEN OVERPAID?

An overpayment is any amount a physician or beneficiary receives in excess of the amount payable under the Medicare program. Physicians are liable for overpayments even if the overpayment is the result of an error by a Medicare carrier (Medicare Carriers Manual [MCM] §§ 7100 & 7103). Except in certain instances where an overpayment is more than 3 years old and was not due to any fault of the physician, overpayments are considered a debt to the United States and must be repaid.

In the scenario above, the Practice's compliance officer should undertake or oversee an organized review of all the claims submitted to Medicare that involve the service in question to verify whether the claims were coded appropriately, and, if not, the extent of an overpayment. Once a physician knows that he or she has been overpaid, the carrier should be notified immediately in writing. The letter should set out the basis for the overpayment, the fact that it was identified through an internal compliance review, and, if possible, identify the patients affected and dates of service. The letter should include a check for the entire amount of the overpayment or, if the practice is not in a position to repay the entire amount, a partial payment should be enclosed with a proposal for making payment over time. Be prepared, however, for the carrier to respond with a demand for financial information relating to the practice's ability to pay, and the imposition of an interest amount on the outstanding balance in excess of 12.625%. Practices would be wise to borrow funds from a bank to avoid burdensome Medicare repayment schedules. Finally, the Practice also must develop a mechanism to refund private payers and patients in connection with improper copayments.

# Investment in an Ambulatory Surgery Center

A gastroenterologist has been offered an opportunity to buy into a local multispecialty ASC. She is offered shares equal to a 10% ownership interest in the ASC and will receive profit distributions consistent with this 10% ownership interest. The per-share price offered to the gastroenterologist is 25% less than the per-share price offered to another physician investor last year. The ASC, consistent with its offerings to other potential physician investors, offers to loan all or part of the purchase price to the gastroenterologist, at 6% interest. The Shareholder Agreement states that there is no requirement that the surgeon perform her surgical procedures at the ASC.

## Does the Proposed Investment in the ASC Constitute a Kickback Violation Under Federal Law?

The principal issue implicated by this scenario is the Federal Anti-Kickback Statute. The Anti-Kickback Statute makes it a criminal offense to knowingly offer or receive remuneration in return for the referral of an individual for the purpose of supplying items or services that may be covered by a federal health care program. "Remuneration" includes anything of value, given directly or indirectly, overtly or covertly, in cash or in kind. In the above scenario, the gastroenterologist will receive items of value from the ASC, in the form of profit distributions, reduced per-share price, and a loan on advantageous terms. She also is in a position to refer procedures to the ASC.

The question, then, is whether the physician's ownership interest would qualify for a safe harbor to the federal statute. Because of the broad language of the of the Federal Anti-Kickback Statute, which could encompass legitimate arrangements that do not present the potential for abuse, Congress authorized the development of regulations, known as *safe harbors*. These safe harbors provide protection for certain conduct that would otherwise violate the statute. Safe harbors have specific requirements, and an arrangement not meeting the requirements exactly will fall outside the protection of the safe harbor. Failure to meet a safe harbor, however, does not necessarily mean that an arrangement is illegal.

There is a particular safe harbor that protects investments in four different types of ASCs. The OIG's overriding theme with the ASC safe harbor is that the ASC should function as an extension of the investing physician's practice. Within that context, there are many complicated requirements, only some of which are discussed below. In particular, there is a safe harbor for ownership in multispecialty ASCs.

The relationships of the previous scenario would not meet an ASC safe harbor for a variety of reasons. First, one of the safe harbor conditions prohibits loans to a potential investor from the entity or other investors for the purpose of investing. Thus, the parties in the above scenario should be aware that if the ASC makes a loan to an investing surgeon, the ASC would no longer fit the safe harbor. Once outside the safe harbor, the loan terms would be examined by the OIG for a determination of whether the terms, such as the low interest rate, are fair market value.

In addition, in the above scenario, the reduced per-share sale price for this particular investor might remove the arrangement from the protection of ASC safe harbor. This is because the amount of payment to an investor in return for the investment must be directly proportional to the amount of the capital investment of that investor. Although at first glance, a profit distribution proportional to the ownership interest would meet this requirement, the reduced per-share price would raise the question of whether the investing gastroenterologist's return is proportional to her capital investment. Failing to meet the safe harbor on this particular issue could be risky because the OIG would be very concerned about the receipt by the gastroenterologist of her shares for less than fair market value, and might view the reduced price to be remuneration in exchange for referrals. This concern could be mitigated, however, if the parties received an independent fair market valuation of the shares before purchase.

As a further condition, one of the relevant ASC safe harbor requirements is that an investing physician who refers procedures to the ASC must derive at least one-third of his or her medical practice income from his or her own performance of surgical procedures that are on the Medicare approved ASC procedure list. In the above scenario, the Shareholder Agreement does not state this as a requirement. In order to ensure that this is the case, the ASC Shareholder Agreement should include this "one-third medical practice" income requirement of all of its physician investors.

Finally, because the ASC is a multispecialty ASC, there is an additional requirement for the physician investors. Specifically, at least one-third of the surgical procedures performed by each physician investor must be performed at the particular ASC in which he or she is investing. In the described scenario, however, the Shareholder Agreement explicitly states that shareholders are not required to refer patients to the ASC. Therefore, the ASC would not meet this safe harbor condition either.

Although a failure to meet the requirements of a safe harbor does not mean that a given arrangement is illegal, the fewer safe harbor requirements that an arrangement meets, the greater the chances of the OIG asserting that the arrangement is abusive.

## MEDICARE CERTIFICATION OF AN AMBULATORY SURGERY CENTER

A group of investors own a multispecialty ASC. The ASC is Medicare certified, and provides services found on the list of Medicare approved ASC procedures list, including colonoscopies. In addition, surgeons at the ASC sometimes perform flexible sigmoidoscopies and other surgical services that are not on the Medicare ASC approved list. The ASC is not as busy as the investors had planned, and in order to generate additional revenue, the investors decide to rent out part of the ASC certified space for several gastroenterologists to perform consults. The leases are at arm's length, reflect fair market value, and fit within the space lease safe harbor.

### CAN LEASING SPACE IN THE ASC TO PHYSICIANS WHO PERFORM NONSURGICAL SERVICES AFFECT THE ASC's CERTIFICATION?

In order to participate in the Medicare program, a facility must meet the Medicare definition of an ASC. The Medicare regulations define an ASC as "any distinct entity that operates exclusively for the purpose of providing surgical services to patients not requiring hospitalization" and that meets other regulatory requirements. If an ASC is not a "distinct entity" or operating "exclusively for the purpose of providing surgical services," as CMS interprets these terms, the ASC will no longer meet the Medicare definition. If a facility no longer meets the Medicare definition of an ASC, the ASC cannot be Medicare certified. If a facility is not Medicare certified, then Medicare will not reimburse the ASC for surgery performed on Medicare patients. Furthermore, some commercial payers may refuse to cover procedures that are not performed at a Medicare certified ASC.

Applying the Medicare definition to the above scenario, the ASC would not meet the Medicare definition of an ASC. By permitting gastroenterologists to lease part of the certified space for consultations, the ASC no longer "operates *exclusively* for the purpose of providing surgical services" (emphasis added). In order to maintain the rental arrangement and meet the definition, the ASC must "carve out" the areas of rented space completely from the certified facility, as long as the "carve out" does not otherwise adversely impact the certification. To avoid uncertainty, inquiry should be made with the appropriate state survey agency.

Until recently, the facts set forth above would have triggered a second issue based on the provision of non-ASC list covered procedures (eg, flex sig) in addition to ASC list covered procedures. Specifically, some officials in CMS had expressed the view that the provision of non-ASC list covered procedures by an ASC also would jeopardize the ASC's Medicare certification. CMS has recently indicated, however, that Medicare certified ASCs may provide surgical services that are not Medicare ASC list procedures. Medicare requires that an ASC be operated for the purpose of providing "*surgical*" services; it is not limited to "covered" surgical services or services on the ASC list.

# CREDIT BALANCES

A gastroenterologist becomes concerned that his practice administrator is not performing adequately and decides to hire a new administrator. The new administrator is asked to evaluate the practice during the first 2 weeks of her employment in a thorough fashion and to report any issues to the gastroenterologist. Two days later, the new administrator comes into the gastroenterologist's office and reports that the practice has accumulated credit balances in the amount of $27,534.32. Some of the credit balances date back as long as 5 years. Apparently, the prior administrator had not instituted any system to return or otherwise dispose of credit balances. The gastroenterologist asks the administrator what should be done.

## HOW SHOULD A PRACTICE TREAT CREDIT BALANCES?

The answer, painful as it may be, is that the practice needs to take steps to return the overpayments. To the extent that the credit balances reflect Medicare and Medicaid services, the Social Security Act makes it a criminal violation of law for any person to fail to disclose or refund a known overpayment of Social Security Act funds, including Medicare or Medicaid monies. Further, the federal government has pursued cases involving credit balances that were taken into income by a provider by alleging that the providers had committed a criminal conversion (or theft) of government property.

Overpayments related to private payer and self-pay services can raise very similar issues. The federal government has taken action against some providers for failing to return copayment and deductible amounts collected in error from Medicare beneficiaries and retained by the providers. Under state law, insurance fraud provisions may, like the Social Security Act, require the disclosure or refund of the overpayments. Private payer agreements may also, as a matter of contract, require the prompt refund of overpayments, such that a state law fraud claim may be brought by a payer whose money is not returned.

Unfortunately, various complications can be encountered when trying to return overpayments. We are aware of situations where Medicare carriers as well as private payers have returned refunded overpayments. In order to prevent being accused later of fraud for failure to make the refund, physicians should send the refund check or offer to make the refund at least twice, in writing, by certified mail. Copies of the letters should be retained in the files for future reference.

Some private payers may have provisions in their provider agreements that make all payment decisions final after a certain period of time, meaning generally that a provider may retain an amount that was paid in error. Physicians are cautioned that failure to refund overpayments *identified* within the prescribed period, but held until after expiration of the time limit for refund, may result in allegations of fraud. If the overpayment is identified only after the period runs, we still suggest considering sending a letter that notifies the payer of the overpayment, but states that the funds will be retained, as permitted by the contract, unless the payer provides documentation to support the repayment.

There also may be problems encountered when a practice tries to make a refund to a patient. A patient may have moved with no forwarding address or, particularly within a Medicare practice, may have died. A practice generally is not entitled to retain a patient overpayment, even under these circumstances. Many states have something called an *escheat law*, where, if a person or entity cannot find the rightful owner of funds or other property after a specified period of time, they are obligated to turn the property over to the state. The state then attempts to find the owner of the property. After a fixed period of time, if the owner has not been located—you guessed it—the state takes the property.

In summary, a practice should take immediate steps to return known overpayments to the appropriate party and should have procedures in place to ensure their prompt identification and refund.

# Sale of Free Samples

Gastroenterology Associates ("GA") is a busy GI practice specializing in endoscopy and colonoscopy. Every year GA receives free drug samples from a pharmaceutical sales representative. The last several years the value of the free samples totaled nearly $6,000. Although GA sometimes gives the free samples to needy patients, it often sells the free samples to patients to help make up for the continuing decline in Medicare payments.

## Is GA at any Legal Risk for Selling the Free Samples to Patients?

Yes, GA may be liable under the Federal Food Drug and Cosmetic Act (FDCA) as well as a state anti-kickback law.

The FDCA is enforced by the US Food and Drug Administration. Section 503(c)(1) of the FDCA prohibits the sale, purchase, or trade or the offer to sell, purchase, or trade drug samples. For purposes of this provision, a drug sample is defined as a unit of drug that is not intended to be sold and is intended to promote the sale of the drug. Drug samples generally are labeled as samples that are not for resale. Violations of the FDCA are punishable by fines and/or imprisonment (FDCA § 303[a] & [b]).

The sale of the free samples to patients also raises significant risk that GA could be liable for receiving an illegal kickback. For example, the Federal Anti-Kickback Statute makes it a crime to knowingly offer, pay, solicit, or receive anything of value (direct or indirect, overt or covert, in cash or in kind) that is intended to induce the referral of a patient for an item or service that is reimbursed by a federal health care program, including Medicare, Medicaid, TRICARE, and the programs covering veterans' benefits (42 USC § 1320a-7b). The law ascribes liability to both sides of an impermissible kickback transaction, and has been interpreted broadly by several courts to apply to situations where only one purpose of a pay-ment is to induce referrals, notwithstanding the fact that there may be other legitimate purposes for which the payment is made.

Traditional application of the Federal Anti-Kickback Statute involves cases where physicians are paid some type of remuneration to refer patients to another health care provider or entity, but the law also applies to a physician or other health care provider who is paid remuneration to prescribe or otherwise recommend a drug that is covered by a federal health care program. Assume, for example, that the facts of the scenario presented are changed so that GA bills either Medicare or Medicaid for the free drug and receives payment. Because GA never paid for the drug, any payments it receives in connection with the samples is tantamount to the pharmaceutical sales representative paying GA cash for prescribing the drug for its patients. Only in this modified scenario, the situation is worse because the federal government unknowingly is the source of the money that is serving as the kickback.

In the scenario set forth above, the Federal Anti-Kickback Statute would not be implicated because GA is not billing a feder-al health care program for the free samples; instead the practice is charging the patients directly. GA, however, is not necessarily free from legal risk. Many states have passed anti-kickback laws that mirror the prohibition found in the federal statute, but which apply to items and services paid for by any payer including the patient (these statutes are referred to as "all-payer" anti-kickback laws). Like the federal statute, these laws may carry civil and/or criminal penalties such as fines and imprisonment or administrative sanc-tions against a physician's medical license.

A gastroenterology practice is located in a small city in a generally rural state. Approximately half of the practice's patients come from the small city and its immediate surrounding areas; the remaining half come from up to 75 miles beyond the city environs. In order to accommodate all of its patients, the practice provides van transportation service. While originally designed for patients from the rural areas, the practice provides the service to any patient who requests it. There is no active promotion of the transportation services by any of the practice's employees. Only after patients have scheduled their appointment with the practice are they asked whether they have transportation services available or whether they need them. However, in its Yellow Pages advertising, there is a picture of the practice's van with the practice's name on the side, and the statement "Transportation Services Available".

## Is it Appropriate to Provide Transportation Services for Patients?

The issue of the propriety of providing transportation services to patients has been debated for many years. Several years ago, at a Congressional hearing, a question was raised to the Inspector General of the Department of Health and Human Services whether such conduct could be considered a violation of the anti-kickback statute. When the Inspector General responded that he did not feel such conduct clearly fit into the prohibitions of the kickback statute, the issue appeared to die. In 1996, however, Congress passed the Health Insurance Portability and Accountability Act (HIPAA), which included, among several anti-fraud and abuse provisions, a section of the law that is known as the Patient Inducement Prohibition. Under HIPAA, it is a civil violation for any provider of services to offer a patient anything of value that the provider knows or should have known would induce the patient to select that provider of services over another. Recognizing that such a broad prohibition could discourage beneficial services that should be encouraged, in the Conference Committee Report accompanying HIPAA, the conferees included language to clarify that the statute was not meant to discourage items of nominal value, such as participation in free health fairs, medical literature, and complimentary local transportation services. The key question to be addressed, therefore, is whether the facts set forth above could be viewed to violate the Patient Inducement Prohibition. The analysis focuses on two issues: (1) Whether the transportation services described qualify as "beneficial services," as presented in the Report language; or (2) whether the transportation services described above could be deemed not to be an inducement and, therefore, does not trigger the statute.

With respect to the beneficial services question, there is, unfortunately, no definition of "local transportation services," nor is there a definition of "nominal" value. While 75 miles would not generally be considered to be "local," if the practice routinely attracts patients from that radius, and 75 miles constitutes the practice's local catchment area, it may qualify as "local." Similarly, while roundtrip cab fare for a 75 mile trip would likely be beyond what is considered a "nominal" amount, a roundtrip bus ticket for the same distance may, in fact, be considered "nominal."

The more important analysis, however, is the question of whether the transportation services described are, in fact, an inducement that could trigger the Patient Inducement Prohibition. To fall under the statute, an inducement likely would require that there be an offer of something of value in order to convince a patient to select a particular practice. In this case, however, the offer of transportation services is made only *after* the patient has already scheduled an appointment with the practice. In such case, it is difficult to argue that the transportation services constituted an inducement. Further, the fact that there is no active promotion of the transportation services by any employee of the practice also supports the position that there is no inducement. The only potential problem is the Yellow Pages advertising. A patient looking for a gastroenterologist in the Yellow Pages may well be influenced to select a particular practice by the availability of transportation services. Therefore, to avoid an allegation that the transportation services constituted a prohibited inducement, the practice should eliminate any reference in their Yellow Pages advertising.

The general issue of providing transportation services to patients has been addressed in an Advisory Opinion published by the Inspector General in November 2000 (OIG Advisory Opinion No. 00-7). In that case, a hospital offered transportation services for a group of patients receiving extended courses of treatment at the hospital. In its opinion approving the services, the OIG identified a series of factors that it considered relevant, including:

- The nature of the free transportation (ie, airline, limousines, or van).
- The geographic area where the services are offered (ie, within or outside of the provider's historic service area).
- Whether the free transportation services are marketed.
- Whether the cost of the services will be claimed directly or indirectly on a federal health care program cost reports.
- The limited availability of publicly available and economical transportation services.

At the same time, the OIG indicated that providing transportation services to all patients is a factor that would not be viewed favorably.

In this case, the modest mode of transportation offered (van service), the limitation to the practice's catchment area, the provision of service to a rural area, the fact that employees do not promote the service, and the fact that the cost of the services are not claimed on a cost report, all support the reasonableness of the services. The practice should, however, eliminate the Yellow Pages advertising to reduce the risk of an allegation of inducement. While it may not be necessary, restricting the availability of services to a group of infirm patients, such as those who have a physical disability, would reduce still further the risk of violating the Patient Inducement Prohibition.

# 41

## MULTIPLE OFFICE GROUP PRACTICE

Nine gastroenterologists, comprising three separate practices, decide to combine together to form a larger group practice. The combined group will continue to practice at all three locations, with three GIs working principally at each of the separate office locations. The members of the group agree that each member shall be compensated on the basis of his or her own individual collections, minus an allocation of the expenses for the office at which they work. In addition, each gastroenterologist will receive the net profits from the radiology services that he or she orders.

## IS THERE ANY LIMITATION ON THE WAY IN WHICH PHYSICIANS CAN STRUCTURE A COMPENSATION RELATIONSHIP WITHIN THEIR PRACTICE?

The major issue for this arrangement is compliance with the Federal Physician Anti-Self-Referral Law, also known as the Stark Law. The Stark Law prohibits physicians from referring Medicare or Medicaid patients for certain "designated health services" to entities with which they have financial relationships. Among the designated health services are radiology services, including magnetic resonance imaging (MRI), computerized axial tomography scans, and ultrasound services.

Under the Stark Law, a physician has made a referral simply by ordering a service. Thus, when physicians order imaging tests, the Stark Law is triggered, and the physicians would be prohibited from making such a referral within the practice unless an exception to the Stark Law applies. The relevant exception is one for the provision of "in-office ancillary service," which requires that the services be provided by or under the supervision of a physician who is a member of the group practice. Although initially this requirement appears simple and straightforward, it is not; the Stark Law has a detailed and restrictive definition of what qualifies as a "group practice."

First, in order to qualify as a Stark "group practice," a practice must function as an integrated, "unified" business and not merely as separate practices bound together in name or referrals alone. In the proposed regulation published by the CMS, this practice's site-by-site allocation of expenses would have caused concern, as CMS had taken the position that an entity could not be a unified business if it shared expenses based on "cost centers." In response to criticism that the proposed regulation would have excluded many bona fide group practices and intruded too far into the financial operations of physician practices, CMS substantially revised the group practice definition in the final rule, and separate cost centers are permitted. However, a group practice still must be organized and operated on a bona fide basis as a single integrated business enterprise with legal and organizational integration, among other requirements. There are additional requirements that would have to be met for the group to qualify as a group practice as well, including:

- Each physician who is a member of the group must furnish substantially the "full range of patient care services" that the physician routinely provides, including medical care, consultation, diagnosis, and treatment, through the joint use of shared office space, facilities, equipment, and personnel.

- At least 75% of the total patient care services of the group practice members must be furnished through the group and billed under a billing number assigned to the group, and the amounts received must be treated as receipts of the group.

- The overhead expenses of, and income from, the practice must be distributed according to methods that are determined before the receipt of payment for the services giving rise to the overhead expense or producing the income.

- Members of the group must personally conduct no less than 75% of the physician-patient encounters of the group practice.

The group practice definition also imposes certain limitations on how physician compensation may be determined. Specifically, the physician members of a group are prohibited from directly receiving compensation based on the volume or value of their own referrals, unless they perform the services themselves or the services are "incident to" the individual physician's services. Applying this limitation to the fact pattern described above, it is acceptable to compensate the physicians based on their collections, reduced by an allocation of expenses to reflect the overhead of their office. Unless the physicians personally perform radiology services, however, because they are designated health services, the proposed compensation methodology is not acceptable under Stark. Instead, profits derived from designated health services should be shared equally among the physician partners, or distributed consistent with each physician's respective ownership in the practice.

# SUPERVISION OF DIAGNOSTIC TESTS

Dr. Dempsey is a solo practitioner. In order to increase the efficiency of her practice and give patients more flexibility in scheduling appointments for diagnostic tests including ultrasounds, Dr. Dempsey schedules her sonographer, Ms. Thomas, to be in the office 5 days a week to perform such tests. Because Dr. Dempsey has tremendous confidence in Ms. Thomas' clinical and technical skills, Dr. Dempsey permits Ms. Thomas to perform these tests while Dr. Dempsey is at the hospital performing endoscopy. One day while scrubbing for her next case, Dr. Dempsey began talking with Dr. Mannon, another gastroenterologist who performs at the same hospital, about the difficulties of running a solo practice and how she relies on Ms. Thomas a great deal. Dr. Mannon informs Dr. Dempsey that based on information he received at a recent lecture on fraud and abuse, he thinks she might be breaking the law by allowing Ms. Thomas to perform the tests when Dr. Dempsey is not in the office.

## IS DR. MANNON CORRECT?

Yes, Dr. Dempsey is violating the Medicare coverage and payment rules as well as the Federal Physician Anti-Self-Referral Act (Stark Law) when she submits claims for the tests she did not supervise directly.

Diagnostic tests covered under Medicare Physician Fee Schedule must be performed, with certain exceptions, under the supervision of a physician and be considered reasonable and necessary, and, therefore, covered by Medicare. The Medicare coverage and payment rules require that ultrasounds be performed under the direct supervision of a physician. This means that in order for test to be payable, the physician must be in the office suite and immediately available to furnish assistance and direction throughout the performance of the procedure.

In addition to the supervision requirement relating to reimbursement, the Stark Law has supervision requirements as well. The Stark Law prohibits a physician from ordering a service that is provided by an entity with which the physician or an immediate family member has a financial relationship if the service falls within one of the categories of designated health services (DHS) covered by the Stark Law and is reimbursed by Medicare or Medicaid, and if the financial relationship does not qualify for an exception. The DHS covered by the law include diagnostic imaging services such as CT scans, MRI, and ultrasound. Penalties for violating the Stark Law include forfeiture of any reimbursement for services rendered based on an unlawful referral, civil fines of up to $15,000 per violation, and exclusion from the Medicare and Medicaid programs.

Because of the broad scope of the Stark Law, Congress exempted certain types of referrals from the self-referral prohibition and authorized the Secretary of the US Department of Health and Human Services to exempt by regulation other arrangements the Department believes pose little fraud and abuse risk. A referral that otherwise implicates the Stark Law must fall within a statutory or regulatory exception or it is per se illegal.

Referrals for a DHS, even if referred within a solo practice, trigger the Stark Law. However, Congress recognized that it may be cost-efficient and convenient for Medicare beneficiaries to obtain certain DHS at their doctor's office, and, therefore, it crafted an exception called the "in-office ancillary services" exception that permits referrals for DHS performed within a physician's own practice. Under this exception, referrals such as the one Dr. Dempsey makes for the ultrasound are permitted so long as a number of criteria are met, including that the DHS must be furnished personally by the referring physician, a member of the same group practice as the referring physician, or *an individual who is supervised by the referring physician* or by another physician in the group practice.

In determining what level of physician supervision, either general, direct, or personal, an individual furnishing a DHS to a Medicare beneficiary must be under for the purpose of meeting the terms of the in-office ancillary services exception, the Stark Law defers to the Medicare coverage and payment rules. Because Medicare has determined that ultrasounds must be performed under a physician's direct supervision in order to be covered, this same standard applies when deciding whether a referral qualifies for the in-office ancillary exception.

The hospital approaches Dr. Smith, a gastroenterologist who is not currently on its medical staff, and offers to make him the medical director of the hospital's new gastroenterology unit at a salary of $100,000 per year plus the use of an administrative assistant on a part-time basis and the use of an office in the hospital. Dr. Smith accepts the offer and begins doing all of his procedures at the hospital. The agreement is not in writing. Dr. Smith's only real service to the hospital is attending staff meetings one evening per month, serving on one hospital committee, and attending semi-annual conferences with the administrative director of the unit.

## IS DR. SMITH AT ANY LEGAL RISK FOR ENTERING INTO THE MEDICAL DIRECTORSHIP ARRANGEMENT?

Dr. Smith is at risk for civil and criminal penalties because the above medical directorship arrangement likely violates the provisions of the Federal Anti-Kickback Statute (42 USC §1320s-7b[b]). The statute prohibits an individual from knowingly and willfully paying remuneration (including any kickback, bribe or rebate) or receiving remuneration in return for referring a patient for a service covered by Medicare or Medicaid. The payer and the receiver of the prohibited remuneration are both held liable under the statute. The purpose of the statute is to prevent unnecessary utilization and to eliminate procedures or services that are not medically necessary, to promote patient choice and prevent arrangements that limit the freedom of the patient to choose a provider, and to reduce costs to federal programs. A person who violates the Federal Anti-Kickback Statute is guilty of a felony and faces fines, imprisonment or both.

There are several statutory exceptions that are known as safe harbors, which the Secretary of Health and Human Services recognizes as specific payment practices that would not trigger criminal prosecution and would not serve as the basis for exclusion from Medicare or Medicaid. The safe harbors include personal and management service contracts between physicians and institutions. The contract or business arrangement must comply with the specific requirements of the safe harbor to be protected.

A medical director agreement must meet the following requirements:

- The agreement must be set out in writing and signed by all involved parties.
- The agreement must specify the services to be provided.
- The agreement must indicate whether the services are provided on a full-time or part-time basis. If services are provided on a part-time basis, the schedule of services and payments for services must be set in advance.
- The term of the agreement must not be less than 1 year.
- The compensation must be set in advance at fair market value, which does not take into account volume or value of referrals between the parties.

The above scenario presents anti-kickback concerns for several reasons. First, the agreement is not in writing. Second, the salary seems to be above fair market value considering that the actual services performed by Dr. Smith are minimal. Finally, it can be presumed that the referral of Dr. Smith's patients to the hospital was a consideration in the decision to appoint him medical director.

## LEASE OF OFFICE SPACE

A surgeon subspecializing in colorectal procedures receives referrals from a gastroenterologist in another part of the county. The patient flow becomes significant enough that the surgeon decides that for the convenience of these patients, he will open a satellite office that he will visit periodically, at least 3 days per month. The most logical location is the office of the gastroenterologist, who has a suite of offices that are not always busy.

The parties sign a lease agreement with the following terms:

- The surgeon will lease office space from the gastroenterologist practice.
- The surgeon will have use of the office 3 days per month, or as the parties may otherwise determine from time to time.
- The rental fee will be $X per each patient seen by the surgeon in the rented space.

The parties did not engage a consultant or otherwise perform an analysis of the fair market value of the space.

### DOES THE LEASE BETWEEN SURGEON AND GASTROENTEROLOGIST PRESENT ANY PROBLEMS?

Any lease between a surgeon and a gastroenterologist who refers to that surgeon will raise questions concerning whether the terms of the lease violate the Federal Anti-Kickback Statute. In fact, in February 2000, the OIG published a special Fraud Alert on the rental of space in physician offices by persons or entities to which the physicians refer. The Fraud Alert identified practices that the OIG believes are "questionable features" of space leases. Among the questionable features identified by the OIG are the rental fees that vary with the number of patients (or referrals). The lease in the described scenario includes such a provision. Because the rental fee varies based on the number of patients seen, the clear incentive for the landlord/gastroenterologist is to refer patients to the surgeon. The OIG would find this to be problematic.

Also, from the facts presented, there is no assurance that the parties established a rental fee that reflects fair market value. An ability to demonstrate the fair market value of the space is crucial to any defense against accusations of impropriety. Another concern relates to the potential variability of the terms of the agreement. Instead of establishing a fixed frequency for the use of the space by the surgeon, use may vary, presumably depending on the volume of patients to be seen.

Fortunately, however, there is a safe harbor that protects lease arrangements meeting certain requirements. The space lease safe harbor requires, generally, that there be a written agreement for at least a 1-year term, and that the agreement covers all of the premises leased between the parties. Further, the aggregate rental charge under the agreement must be set in advance, reflect fair market value for the space, and may not vary with the volume or value of referrals between the parties. In addition, the aggregate space leased may not exceed a commercially reasonable amount given the business purpose of the agreement. Finally, if the lease is a part-time lease, the agreement must specify exactly the schedule or intervals, and state the exact rent for such intervals.

Metropolitan Gastroenterology, P.C. ("MG") and Digestive Health Associates, P.C. ("DHA") both own and operate an ASC to enhance the profitability of their group practices. The physicians in both groups realize, however, that their geographic area will not sustain two ASCs. As a result, the groups decide to enter into a joint venture to own and operate one ASC, called Metro Healthplex, Inc. ("MH"). The terms of the joint venture call for the gastroenterologists of both practices to own equal shares of MH and for the distribution of any profits to be divided according to referrals to the optical shop. Both practices include Medicare patients. Net profits related to business generated from other sources will be disbursed equally across all the physician owners.

## DOES THE PROPOSED JOINT VENTURE POSE ANY LEGAL RISK FOR THE PHYSICIAN-OWNERS?

Yes. The Federal Physician Anti-Self-Referral law (Stark law) prohibits a physician from ordering a service that is provided by an entity with which the physician or an immediate family member has a financial relationship if the service falls within one of the categories of DHS covered by the Stark law and is reimbursed by Medicare or Medicaid, and if the financial relationship does not qualify for an exception (42 USC § 1395nn). Surgical and diagnostic procedures typically performed by a gastroenterologist in an ASC setting fall within the definition of DHS. Consequently, unless the ASC arrangement fell within one of the Stark law exceptions, referrals of patients to the ASC with which the physician had an investment or compensation relationship would violate the Stark law.

In addition to the legal concerns raised by the Stark law, ASC joint ventures involving physicians who are both investors in the joint venture and who are in a position to refer to the joint venture may raise concerns under the Federal Anti-Kickback Statute. To the extent that gastroenterologists may profit from referrals of patients to ASCs in which the gastroenterologists have a financial interest, the Federal Anti-Kickback Law may be triggered.

The Federal Anti-Kickback Statute prohibits the offer, solicitation, payment, or receipt of anything of value (direct or indirect, overt or covert, in cash or in kind) that is intended to induce the referral of a patient for an item or service that is reimbursed by a federal health care program, including Medicare or Medicaid. The law imposes liability to both sides of an impermissible kickback transaction, and has been interpreted broadly by several courts to apply to situations where only one purpose of a payment is to induce referrals, notwithstanding the fact that there may be other legitimate purposes for which the payment is made. As a result, virtually any financial relationship in which a health care provider is a referral source, as is the case here, has potential anti-kickback implications.

Because this law, as drafted, would prohibit many practical and nonabusive ways of delivering health care, Congress adopted several exceptions to the law and granted the OIG of the Department of Health and Human Services authority to except additional arrangements from the reach of the law through regulations called safe harbors. These safe harbors define practices that are not subject to the Federal Anti-Kickback Statute because they are viewed by the government as being unlikely to result in fraud and abuse. Unfortunately, because of the narrow manner in which the safe harbor regulations are drafted, the existing safe harbors offer no protection under the presented facts. Failure to fit within a safe harbor, however, does not mean that an arrangement is per se illegal. Therefore, one must look to other guidance to determine the degree of risk involved.

One source of information is a publication by the OIG known as a Fraud Alert. Fraud Alerts are statements of the OIG's view on certain common arrangements. In 1989, the OIG issued a Special Fraud Alert on Joint Venture Arrangements under the Anti-Kickback law

("Fraud Alert") discussing joint venture arrangements that may violate the Federal Anti-Kickback law. Though 15 years old, the document still remains useful for identifying factors of various investment structures that may increase or decrease liability under the Anti-Kickback law. The Fraud Alert identified three principal areas that the OIG would review when analyzing joint ventures: (1) the manner in which investors are selected, (2) the nature of the business structure of the arrangement, and (3) the financing and profit distributions. Specifically, the Fraud Alert identified the following "red flags" as indicators of potentially unlawful activity:

1. Investors are chosen because they are in a position to make referrals.

2. Physicians who are expected to make a large number of referrals may be offered a greater investment opportunity in the joint venture than those anticipated to make fewer referrals.

3. Physician investors may be actively encouraged to make referrals to the joint venture and may be encouraged to divest their ownership interest if they fail to sustain an acceptable level of referrals.

4. The joint venture tracks its sources of referrals and distributes this information to the investors.

5. Investors may be required to divest their ownership interest if they cease to practice in the service area, for example, if they move, become disabled, or retire.

6. Investment interests are nontransferable.

7. The structure of the joint venture may be suspect, such as in the case of a "shell entity." A shell entity is identified as one where there is very little capital, equipment, or other hard assets in the venture and another entity is responsible for the day to day operations of the joint venture.

8. The amount of capital invested by the physician is disproportionately small and the return disproportionately large compared to a typical investment in a new business.

9. Physician investors only invest a nominal amount, such as $500 to $1500.

10. Investors are permitted to borrow the amount of the investment from the entity and pay it back through deductions from profit distributions.

11. Investors may be paid extraordinary returns on the investment in comparison to the risks involved, often well over 50% to 100% per year.

While the ASC joint venture likely avoids many of the concerns set forth in the Fraud Alert, there is one issue that should be addressed. In particular, the investors should not receive distributions based on the volume of their referrals to the business, but rather based solely on their equity ownership in MH. Other ways to reduce risk include extending investment opportunities to nonreferral sources.

# THE HEALTH INSURANCE PORTABILITY AND ACCOUNTABILITY ACT OF 1996 (HIPAA): COMPLIANCE AND BUSINESS ASSOCIATES

A gastroenterology practice hires a software vendor to install and implement a new software program that will transfer the practice's current patient record electronic filing system into a software program utilizing a more organized and easily accessible format. The software vendor intends to market its product by producing a website that allows potential customers to view how the product has been used to update its current clients' information systems.

## IS THE SOFTWARE VENDOR A "BUSINESS ASSOCIATE" UNDER THE HIPAA PRIVACY RULE?

Yes, if the vendor has access to protected health information (PHI). A "business associate" is a person or organization, other than a member of a covered entity's workforce, which uses identifiable health information to perform certain functions or activities for a covered entity. Such functions might include claims processing, data analysis, financial services, and billing. Persons or organizations are not considered business associates if their functions or services do not involve the use or disclosure of PHI, and where any access to PHI by such persons would be incidental, if at all.

In this example, the vendor will not be considered a business associate if it is merely selling or providing software to the practice and does not have access to the practice's PHI. However, if the vendor does need access to PHI in order to provide its service, the vendor would be considered a business associate of the practice. Thus, if the vendor maintains the software containing patient information on its own server or needs to access the practice's patient information when troubleshooting software malfunctions, it is a business associate of the practice, and the practice must enter into a business associate agreement with the vendor before allowing the vendor to access PHI.

This business associate agreement is a contract that provides certain protections of PHI. Through this contract, the covered entity must obtain a commitment from business associates that meets the following requirements:

- Not use or disclose PHI other than as permitted by the agreement or required by law.
- Use appropriate safeguards to protect the confidentiality of the information.
- Report to the covered entity any use or disclosure not permitted by the agreement.
- Ensure agreement by any agents or subcontractors to the same restrictions and conditions as the business associate.
- Make available to the covered entity the information as necessary for it to comply with the patients' rights to access, amend and receive an accounting of disclosures of their PHI.
- Make available to the Secretary of the Department of Health and Human Services the business associate's internal practices, books, and records relating to the use and disclosure of PHI.
- Return or destroy the information once the contract is terminated, if feasible.

In this example, the practice must impose specified written safeguards on the individually identifiable health information used or disclosed by the vendor. Moreover, the practice may not contractually authorize the vendor to make any use or disclosure of protected health information that would violate the HIPAA Privacy Rule.

# ARRANGEMENTS FOR THE PROVISION OF CLINICAL LABORATORY SERVICES

Gastroenterology Associates ("GA") seeks to retain the services of Specimens, Inc., a local laboratory. The practice wants to focus on building a comfortable and convenient environment for its patients, and thus accepts the laboratory's offer for the provision of on-site phlebotomy services. The phlebotomist would collect specimens for GA, and also help the practice's office staff by taking vital signs and performing clerical services. The laboratory has also offered, free of charge, to pick up and dispose of biohazardous waste products unrelated to the laboratory's usual collection of specimens.

## CAN THE PRACTICE ESTABLISH THIS BUSINESS RELATIONSHIP WITH THE LABORATORY?

No, because the practice might be in violation of the Federal Anti-Kickback Statute. The Federal Anti-Kickback Statute makes it a crime to receive anything of value that is offered for the purpose of inducing the referral of a patient for a service that is reimbursed by a federal health care program.

While it is permissible for a practice to rely on the services of outside clinical laboratories, the problem lies with the extent to which a practice, a referral source for the laboratory, accepts any service of the laboratory without paying fair market value for the services. "Fair market value" means value for general commercial purposes, and reflects an arms-length transaction that has not been adjusted to include the additional value that either or both parties has attributed to the referral of business between them. If the practice accepts services that it would otherwise pay for if they solicited these services elsewhere, the inference may be made that the services were offered to induce the referral of business to the laboratory. The practice would be in violation of the Federal Anti-Kickback

Statute whether or not it solicited the services; merely accepting the services from the laboratory would constitute a violation of the statute.

## The On-Site Phlebotomist

If permitted by state law, a laboratory can offer the services of an on-site phlebotomist who collects specimens from patients for testing by the outside laboratory. While the mere placement of a laboratory employee in the practice's office would not, in itself, amount to an inducement prohibited by the statute, the statute is implicated when the phlebotomist performs additional tasks not directly related to the collection or processing of laboratory specimens. In the present example, the phlebotomist's performance of these additional tasks creates a strong inference that he or she is providing a benefit in return for the practice's referrals to the laboratory. If these arrangements were established to induce the referral of laboratory testing reimbursable under a federal health care program, then the practice may be liable under the statute and may be subject to criminal prosecution and exclusion from participation in such programs.

## Free Pick Up and Disposal of Biohazardous Waste Products Unrelated to the Laboratory's Usual Collection of Specimens

In the above example, the practice may likely have exposure under the Anti-Kickback Statute if the practice accepts these free services. As with the phlebotomist, the inference may be made that the free service was offered to induce the referral of business to the laboratory.

# INDIVIDUAL RIGHTS UNDER THE HIPAA PRIVACY RULE

Mr. Phillips had just completed his office visit with Dr. Peterson, the gastroenterologist who Mr. Phillips sees periodically for treatment of GERD, when he said to Dr. Peterson "And by the way, I'd like to get from you a listing of all the people you've sent any of my medical information to for the last 5 years." A very surprised Dr. Peterson said he was pretty sure that his office didn't track such disclosures but would do the best he could.

## DOES DR. PETERSON HAVE TO COMPLY WITH THE PATIENT'S REQUEST?

Yes. The final privacy rule, promulgated under the authority of HIPAA, brings an unprecedented level of federal protection to personal health information. One essential element of meaningful privacy protection is the ability of an individual to access and control his or her own personal health information. The final privacy rule requires a covered entity to provide adequate notice to an individual regarding the entity's use and disclosure of protected health information (PHI), as well as of the individual's rights with respect to such information. In the required notice, covered entities must describe certain rights available to individuals, including the right to request restrictions on uses and disclosures, the right to receive confidential communications of PHI, the right to inspect and copy PHI, the right to amend PHI, and the right to an accounting of disclosures of PHI. Covered entities include health plans, health care clearinghouses, and health care providers who transmit health information in electronic form in connection with a standard transaction. PHI includes information that identifies the patient and (1) relates to the patient's past, present or future physical or mental health or condition; (2) addresses the health services, diagnosis or treatment provided to the patient; or (3) addresses the billing or payment for services provided to the patient.

## Right to Inspect and Copy PHI

The privacy rule grants individuals a right of access to PHI that is maintained in a designated records set. However, covered entities may deny individuals access to otherwise accessible information, without an opportunity for review, in certain situations. First, access is not required, but may be provided in the case of psychotherapy notes; information compiled in reasonable anticipation of a civil, criminal or administrative proceeding; and certain PHI that is subject to or exempted from the Clinical Laboratory Improvements Amendments of 1988. Second, a covered entity may temporarily deny an individual access to PHI that was obtained by a covered provider in the course of research for as long as the research is in progress. This exception is conditioned on the individual's having agreed to the denial of access in conjunction with the research trial consent and the covered provider's having informed the individual of the right of access to the information upon completion of the research. Third, a covered entity may deny access to PHI that is subject to the Privacy Act (5 USC 552a) if such denial is permitted under the Privacy Act. And fourth, an individual's access may be denied if the PHI was obtained from someone other than a health care provider under a promise of confidentiality and the access requested would be reasonably likely to reveal the source of the information. This provision was intended to protect a covered entity's ability to agree to maintain certain information as confidential.

The privacy rule provides three additional grounds to deny an individual access; however, in these cases, the individual has the right to have the denial reviewed by a licensed health care professional who is designated by the covered entity to act as a reviewing official and who did not participate in the original decision to deny. First, covered entities may deny an individual access to PHI if a licensed health care professional has determined that the access is likely to endanger the life or physical safety of that individual or another person (eg, demonstration of homicidal or suicidal tendencies). Second, covered entities may deny access if the information requested makes reference to someone other than the individual and a licensed health care professional has determined that the access is reasonably likely to cause serious harm to that other person. Third, covered entities may deny access if the request is made by the individual's personal representative and a licensed health care professional has determined that access to such representative is reasonably likely to cause substantial harm to the individual or another person (eg, in cases where the individual may be subject to domestic violence, abuse, or neglect by the personal representative). It is important to note that, after denying access to PHI, a covered entity must still provide the individual with access to any remaining (nondeniable) requested PHI.

Covered entities must act within 30 days of receiving a request for access if the information is maintained or accessible on-site, and within 60 days if located off-site, with both periods subject to a possible 30-day extension. Access under the privacy rule includes the ability of an individual to both inspect and obtain a copy of PHI in designated health sets. Covered entities may charge a reasonable, cost-based fee for copying information (including labor and supply costs), but may not charge any fees for retrieving the information or processing the request.

### Right to Receive Confidential Communications of PHI

Individuals may also request that covered entities provide communications of PHI in a confidential manner, such as by sending information by alternative means or to alternative locations. For example, if an individual does not want certain family members to know about his or her treatment, that individual could request that communications regarding the treatment only be sent to the individual's place of employment or enclosed in an envelope rather than sent by a postcard. Unlike the restriction requests discussed above where a covered entity may categorically deny such requests, covered health care providers must accommodate all reasonable requests for confidential communications. Health plans must also accommodate reasonable requests if the individual clearly states that the disclosure of the PHI could endanger him or her.

## Right to Request Restrictions of Uses and Disclosures

The final rule permits individuals to request that covered entities restrict the use and disclosure of PHI. However, covered entities are not required to agree to any such restrictions. If a covered entity does agree to a restriction, then except in certain emergency situations, it may not use or disclose PHI in violation of such restriction. For example, if an individual requests that a covered entity never disclose PHI to a particular family member (even if such disclosure would otherwise be permissible), the covered entity must never disclosure PHI to this family member provided that it has agreed to abide by such restriction.

A covered entity may terminate a restriction with the individual's written or oral agreement. Oral agreements must be documented, such as by a note in the medical record. A covered entity may terminate a restriction without the individual's agreement, but the termination will only affect PHI created or received by the covered entity after the individual is informed of the termination.

## Right to Accounting of Disclosures of PHI

Except in limited cases, individuals also have the right to receive an accounting of disclosures of PHI made by a covered entity in the 6 years prior to the request. Covered entities must exclude disclosures to a health oversight agency or law enforcement official if inclusion of the disclosure would be reasonably likely to impede the activities of the agency or official. The accounting must contain a brief statement of the purpose of the disclosure and must reasonably inform the individual of the basis for the disclosure. Covered entities are required to provide the accounting within 60 days after receipt of the request, subject to a possible 30-day extension. Individuals have the right to receive from each covered entity one free accounting per 12-month period.

## Right to Amend PHI

The privacy rule also provides individuals with the right to have a covered entity amend PHI and records in a designated record set for as long the information is maintained in the set. The rule permits a covered entity to deny a request only if the entity did not create the PHI or record that is subject to the request, the requested PHI is not part of a designated record set, the information would not otherwise be available for inspection, or the disputed information is accurate and complete. Covered entities are required to respond to requests for amendment within 60 days, subject to a possible 30-day extension.

Covered entities that accept an individual's request for amendment must make the amendment, but they are not required to expunge any PHI. If an entity denies a request for amendment, it must provide the individual with a written statement of denial. The denial must include the basis for such denial, information on how to file a statement in disagreement of the denial, and how the individual may make a complaint.

# OFFICE OF INSPECTOR GENERAL'S COMPLIANCE GUIDANCE FOR INDIVIDUAL AND SMALL GROUP PHYSICIAN PRACTICES

On September 25, 2000, the OIG of the US Department of Health and Human Services published its *Compliance Guidance for Individual and Small Group Physician Practices* 65 Fed. Reg. 59434 (Oct. 5, 2000). In keeping with the OIG's earlier publications of compliance guidance for institutional health care providers such as hospitals, skilled nursing facilities, and home health agencies, the physician practice guidelines address the seven elements of an effective compliance program described in *US Sentencing Commission Guidelines for Organizations*. The function of an effective compliance program is to establish a formal process for submitting complete and accurate claims to third-party payers, to establish procedures designed to deter potential illegal conduct, and to establish a mechanism for responding to audits and detected violations of the law.

Physician practices, like all health care providers, are subject to a broad array of federal laws and regulations when they participate in any federally funded program such as Medicare. In the *Compliance Guidance for Individual and Small Group Physician Practices*, the OIG has highlighted several risk areas, including the following:

- Advance beneficiary notices, which place patients on notice that particular services may not be covered under Medicare.
- Physician compliance with the prerequisites for certifying the need for home health care services or durable medical equipment.
- Physician obligations under the Emergency Medical Treatment and Active Labor Act (EMTALA).
- Gainsharing agreements between physicians and hospitals.
- Third-party billing practices and agreements.
- Professional courtesy.

- Physician incentive agreements.
- Agreements for personal services or rentals of office space.

## ADMINISTRATIVE FLEXIBILITY

Unlike the OIG's previous compliance guidelines, the physician practice guidelines allow for more flexibility in two significant respects. First, the guidelines contain a relaxed standard for implementing a compliance program. Based on its size, resources, and relevant risk factors, a practice may choose to rely on selective portions of the guidelines in crafting a compliance program tailored to meet its needs, or may elect to implement components of a full compliance program on a piecemeal basis.

These guidelines adopt an operational approach to compliance, which suggests a series of steps that physician practices can take when phasing in a compliance program. They attempt to draw a distinction between billing errors caused by inadvertence or negligence, and those errors caused by reckless or intentional conduct, which may trigger multiple damages and fines under the False Claims Act, administrative sanctions by the OIG, or may violate criminal laws. While the OIG states that all physicians have a duty to ensure that all claims they submit are accurate and complete, the more severe sanctions are reserved for reckless or intentional conduct. Even though the OIG's discussion of these standards is commendable, the line between honest or negligent mistakes and those errors that involve actual knowledge, deliberate ignorance, or reckless disregard of Medicare and Medicaid billing rules is often blurry, and frequently will depend on the facts of each case. As a result, because the sanctions available to the OIG can be so severe, physicians and physician groups should carefully evaluate those practices that pose a risk under any health care program.

## KEY ELEMENTS OF THE
## PHYSICIAN COMPLIANCE GUIDANCE

The elements of the guidelines are similar to those for larger and more complex providers. Nevertheless, the OIG also recommends that portions of a compliance program may be borrowed from existing programs adopted by other entities with which the physician has regular contact, such as a local hospital. In addition, a physician practice may also take advantage of educational opportunities offered through such institutions. In order to avoid potential violations of the Federal Anti-Kickback Statute, the guidelines discourage physician practices from using hospitals as sources for other compliance tasks, unless fair market value is provided for those services. Regardless of the form selected, the program must meet the needs of the specific practice to be effective; a template or generic program may do more harm than good.

## 1. Auditing and Monitoring

A successful compliance program requires comprehensive information about a practice and how it submits claims to third-party payers. An essential part of developing a compliance program is a review of existing procedures through an internal audit. These baseline audits should focus on factors that contribute to billing errors, such as proper documentation of medical necessity and services rendered, proper coding, and the presence of improper financial incentives. No single audit method is required; the practice may choose to review a random sample of claims, or may want to review claims covering those services that are particularly troublesome. If any problems are identified during a baseline audit, the practice will be able to address them as part of developing the compliance program through remedial action, including any overpayment refunds.

In addition to conducting baseline audits, the practice should also strongly consider conducting follow-up audits on a regular basis to measure the strengths and weaknesses of the compliance program. As with baseline audits, these audits can examine a randomly selected sample of claims, or can focus on areas identified as posing a special risk based on the practice's past history or on external factors such as information regarding government investigations of similarly situated practices or agency workplans.

## 2. Practice Standards and Procedures

The heart of any compliance program is the code of conduct that the organization adopts that includes its commitment to complying with the law and an expectation that every employee, agent, or contractor affiliated with the organization will adhere to that code and understand that it will be a factor in evaluating that individual's performance.

No single format for a code of conduct is prescribed in the OIG's guidelines. Some practices may find it economical to adopt parts of existing compliance standards developed by the entities with which they are affiliated, such as hospitals or physician networks. However, these standards should be tailored to fit the exact needs of the practice. In addition, the OIG has also recommended that an alternative to developing a code of conduct for the practice is to create a central repository for procedure manuals and publications distributed by HCFA and the OIG.

Regardless of the format selected by the practice, the OIG has recommended that the code of conduct at least address four important risk areas:

- Coding and billing, to ensure that the claims submitted are accurate, use appropriate modifiers, and do not violate rules prohibiting unbundling or upcoding.
- Verifying that services are reasonable and necessary.
- Ensuring that the documentation supports the services provided to the beneficiary, which includes both the content of the physician's medical record as well as the information entered on a HCFA-1500 claim form.
- Avoiding improper inducements, kickbacks, and self-referrals. This concern covers agreements between the physician and other health care providers or suppliers, which may trigger the Anti-Kickback or self-referral law, and improper beneficiary incentives, such as waivers of copayments.

As part of developing standards of conduct, the OIG recommends that the practice implement a system of retaining important documents relating to its compliance activities in addition to record retention requirements already mandated under federal and state law. The documents that should be retained can include reference materials on compliance, the practice's own compliance records, and information received from external sources. This last category can include such items as correspondence to and from third-party payers and Medicare carriers regarding compliance with billing procedures. Such records may prove helpful in an audit or investigation to help establish that the practice was making a good faith effort to comply with the law, and can reduce the possibility of severe penalties in the event of any overpayment.

## 3. Designating a Compliance Officer or Contact

A successful compliance program requires that there be responsibility for the day to day operations of the program. Because individual and small group practices often lack the resources to designate a full-time compliance officer, the OIG has suggested that this function can be delegated to several individuals within the practice; another option is to retain an external compliance officer. Each option should be carefully examined to determine the best and most efficient arrangement for a specific practice.

The responsibilities of the compliance officer or committee include the following:

- Overseeing the implementation of the compliance program.
- Establishing methods to improve the efficiency and quality of services, and to minimize the risk of fraud and abuse violations.
- Reviewing and revising the program to conform to changes in the law, and changes in reimbursement policies.
- Developing and executing training programs on compliance issues.
- Ensuring that employees, independent contractors, and agents retained by the practice are aware of its compliance policies and have not been the subject of prior sanctions or convictions relating to health care or government-funded programs.
- Implementing policies to encourage confidential reports of problems or suspected violations.
- Conducting internal investigations in response to any such reports and adopting appropriate corrective actions.

## 4. Appropriate Training and Education

Even the best-crafted compliance program cannot be fully implemented without comprehensive training and education of all staff who have any impact on the practice's ability to provide services in accord with relevant law. Accordingly, the guidelines recommend that educational programs be offered to all staff. The programs can take a variety of forms, including in-service training, attendance at compliance seminars, and training offered by providers affiliated with the practice. The OIG recommends that the training be focused on providing staff with the tools needed to understand how to perform their jobs in accordance with relevant laws, regulations, and policies. In addition, the OIG expects that the training will make the staff aware that compliance is a part of their job description and evaluation. In addition to basic training, the OIG further recommends that supplemental training may be necessary for all staff with responsibility for coding and billing, particularly if the practice does not employ a certified coder. For those practices that rely on external billing companies, the practice should ensure that the company adheres to the guidelines established by the OIG for third-party billing companies.

## 5. Responding to Detected Offenses and Corrective Action Plans

No compliance plan can guarantee that offenses will not occur in the future; therefore, a good plan will establish a mechanism for responding appropriately to offenses discovered as the result of compliance activities. In many instances, the practice's response to an alleged violation can be the most significant step in establishing that it is reliable and trustworthy.

The OIG's guidelines emphasize the need for a prompt response by the practice to suspected violations of the law, and to implement corrective actions when violations are detected. The need for prompt action can be triggered by information received from employees or patients; it can also be the product of internal audits or warning signals identified by the practice, including a pattern or an overall increase in denied claims, a significant change in claims submitted to carriers and third-party payers, or specific correspondence from carriers and third-party payers concerning coding and billing practices.

Regardless of the origin of the practice's concern, the OIG emphasizes that any internal investigation must be rigorous. If the investigation uncovers a violation, the practice must then take the necessary steps to ensure that the violation is not compounded. This can include such remedial actions as amending the compliance program, a disclosure to the carrier or to the government, and appropriate disciplinary action for the individuals involved in the misconduct. The response of the practice will turn on the specific facts of the case, and may require careful consultation with counsel as to the best course of action. Even though this guidance from the OIG may appear strict, the agency notably avoided suggesting that physicians or groups notify government agencies of suspected violations while investigations were still being conducted, as it had in its compliance guidelines for some institutional providers.

## 6. Developing Open Lines of Communication

A significant aspect of an effective compliance program is the ability of the employees and agents of a health care provider to report suspected illegal conduct without fear of retaliation. This is particularly true with small physician practices. The OIG guidelines expand on this concept by encouraging an informal process that allows for an exchange of information among the physicians, compliance personnel, and other staff. This type of exchange can cover all aspects of a compliance program, with particular emphasis on reports of suspected fraud, waste, or abuse, or requests for clarification of appropriate procedures or relevant legal requirements. Although practices are free to develop their own internal criteria, the OIG's guidelines list the following suggestions for promoting open communication:

- Requiring that employees report conduct that may be erroneous or fraudulent if the employee has a good faith belief that the information is accurate.
- Informing employees that a failure to report fraudulent conduct is a violation of their obligations under the compliance program.
- Developing a simple process to handle reports of suspected misconduct.
- If the practice uses a billing company, establishing regular contacts with that company's compliance officer to coordinate compliance activities.

- Informing employees that they may report suspected conduct anonymously, although the employees should be cautioned that their anonymity cannot be guaranteed if the report results in a government investigation or in litigation.
- Assuring employees that the practice's code of conduct prohibits any retribution for reporting conduct that a reasonable person acting in good faith would believe is fraudulent or erroneous.

## 7. Enforcing Disciplinary Standards Through Well-Publicized Guidelines

A compliance program cannot be truly effective without enforcement of the practice's code of conduct through appropriate and consistent disciplinary mechanisms that are publicized to all employees of the practice. The consistency of the enforcement is a key element in ensuring that employees and agents understand the practice's commitment to compliance with the law. In addition, such actions also demonstrate the practice's commitment to government authorities should it be investigated by a government agency such as the OIG.

The precise form of discipline must depend on the nature, extent, and duration of any misconduct. This process can be flexible enough to take into account relevant mitigating and aggravating factors. The sanctions selected can range from oral or written warnings to temporary suspension or restitution of damages, and can be as severe as termination of employment. However the disciplinary remedy is enforced, it must be enforced consistently without any discrimination based on factors such as a job title or supervisory responsibility.

## CHOOSING THE RIGHT COMPLIANCE TRAINING FOR YOUR PRACTICE

Gastroenterology Associates, P.C. ("GA") is a large metropolitan-based, multioffice practice. It has made a serious commitment to compliance, but has been less than effective in making sure that its many staff members are fully aware of the internal policies and procedures under GA's compliance plan.

## WHAT ARE GA'S OPTIONS FOR EFFECTIVE COMPLIANCE TRAINING?

Regardless of the size of your practice, there are a seemingly infinite number of rules and regulations involved in the business of modern medicine. You sincerely want your organization to do things "the right way", but how do you ensure that this message gets delivered to the billers, coders, nurses, technicians, and staff that make up your organization?

Your organization's compliance with the regulatory morass will depend on both the timing as well as the adequacy of the education and training received by all of the individuals involved. As discussed in the previous chapter, the OIG views training as a crucial component of any organization's compliance efforts. But who should do the training? When should the training be done, and how frequently? What kind of training does your organization need?

### Issues to Consider in Deciding on Timing of Training

If your organization is committed to compliance, then it has or is planning on conducting both compliance training as well as a compliance audit. A compliance audit essentially is a systematic review of an organization's regulatory vulnerabilities. A question that frequently does not receive much attention is whether the compliance training should be conducted before or after the compliance audit.

The "when" may not seem to be an important issue. However, the timing of the training can have important implications.

## Training Before Auditing

Conducting training prior to conducting a baseline compliance audit can make sense for some organizations, though it clearly won't for others. A potential advantage of a "training first" approach includes the possible psychological benefit of putting a nonthreatening face on the initial compliance efforts in a way that makes individual and organizational buy-in an easier sell. In some cases, however, if not handled properly a pretraining audit can turn the subsequent training session into a punitive, finger-pointing exercise that will turn sensitive personnel off to compliance efforts. For some organizations, a "training first" approach gives the organization a chance to put a subsequent audit in a "big picture" context that is comforting and encourages a receptive response (or at least not an overtly hostile one).

An additional reason why some organizations find it in their best interest to train first is that it may reduce the overpayment liability that can come with initiating a compliance program. To the extent that you view training as the activity that is most likely to get your entity "doing things right," you and your organization can't set up your training program fast enough. With an "audit first" approach, some organizations fret about the time that it will take between conducting the audit and translating the findings into a focused training program with the chance to change behavior, leaving potentially noncompliant behaviors in place and exposing the practice to continuing risk.

## Auditing Before Training

Despite the arguments to be made for a "training first" approach (which clearly is the best approach for some organizations), there is ample support for conducting a baseline compliance audit prior to training. This is because, despite some of the advantages of conducting training first, many think the most significant advantage of the baseline audit is that it will clarify your compliance issues and bring a focus to every component of your compliance activities that follow—including the training.

Once a baseline audit has been conducted and a report has been issued, your organization's compliance vulnerabilities will be clear (or at least a lot clearer). The audit report should identify corrective actions and, in most instances, adequate training will be a significant component of that corrective action. Using the audit report as a training roadmap will ensure that the training and your training resources are not squandered on "issues" that are not problems for your practice. This also means that staff are much less likely to dismiss training sessions as a "waste of time." Experience indicates that employees' psychological "buy-in" with regard to compliance is highly dependent on the credibility and efficiency of the entire exercise, including the educational components.

Another factor to consider is that one of the most effective compliance training techniques involves factual scenarios. The advantage of conducting training after the completion of the compliance audit is clear: the factual "scenarios" will be real and therefore the examples will hit home. Employees who may have believed that there are no potential issues in their department will now know otherwise and be less likely to dismiss the training. It becomes much harder for employees to disregard the training after a baseline audit has brought potential compliance issues to light.

One often-disregarded reason for conducting the training only after the audit has been completed is the risk of actually creating your own whistleblower. Essentially, by conducting the training without knowing whether a practice has a particular vulnerability (and thus without making sure that the practice has a corrective plan in place), the training session can uncover—in a clumsy way—compliance problem after compliance problem without any means of containing the damage.

## Issues to Consider in Choosing a Compliance Training Approach

There are a variety of issues that must be considered before hiring a compliance trainer or adopting a particular compliance training approach. In other words, even after you have answered the question as to "when" to train, you have to ask yourself the question about "how" you should train.

The basic question is whether an internal employee familiar with compliance issues should do the training or whether the organization should hire an outside professional with compliance expertise and training experience. In evaluating who should do the training, compliance officers or other decision makers should consider the following: flexibility in scheduling, cost, reproducibility and frequency, ease of documentation and familiarity with sensitive documentation issues, ability to update, and maximizing the educational opportunity for the persons most responsible for internal compliance efforts.

## Internal vs External Trainer

As might be expected, the OIG acknowledges that the use of both internal and external trainers can be appropriate. Determining what is best for your organization will depend, at least in part, on the size and resources of the practice. For some entities, the cost of engaging an external trainer may be prohibitive. Other entities may feel they have sufficient internal resources (compliance officers, billing and coding experts) to eliminate the need for an external professional. In all cases, however, practices should be aware of the advantages and disadvantages of each option.

To be sure, a compliance trainer from within the practice or entity has advantages in terms of cost, flexible scheduling, and the ability to repeat the training as needed. In many cases, the external persons or company with the necessary specific expertise will not be local, necessitating travel (with its attendant costs). With an external professional trainer, the training will have to be done on his or her schedule, and finding a mutually acceptable date and time often can be time-consuming. The ability to repeat the training may, therefore, be limited and costly, as refresher courses or training for new employees will necessitate additional travel and expense. Fortunately, this additional cost may be obviated by the use of videotape.

Despite some disadvantages in terms of cost and flexibility, external trainers are usually the trainers of choice, particularly with respect to initial and more significant subsequent training programs. This is because—rightly or wrongly—it often takes an external expert to lend credibility to the compliance enterprise. The fact of the matter is that employees frequently perceive external trainers as more credible than internal personnel with whom they work on a daily basis. Often, a credentialed external professional is more likely to engage the attention of the practice's trainees.

There are additional advantages to hiring an external professional to conduct the training. External professional compliance trainers are far more likely to be sensitive to the important documentation issues that confront a practice embarking upon a compliance program. In addition, by hiring an external professional trainer, the entity's own compliance professionals are able to avail themselves of the educational opportunity.

## What Are the Different Types of Training and What Is Best for My Organization?

There are a variety of types of compliance training. Often, the choice of trainer will dictate the type of training. Likewise, the type of desired training may dictate the choice of trainer. The method that works best will depend greatly on the type, size, and resources of the organization.

Some important factors to consider include:

- *Trainee engagement:* The effectiveness of a compliance program is highly dependent on whether the staff is engaged in the exercise.
- *Credibility of the trainer or training approach:* This (perceived or actual) is crucial for the buy-in of the entire organization. Third-party vendors tend to be perceived by employees as more credible.
- *Cost*
- *Reproducibility:* Can the training be reproduced easily for new hires and to meet "refresher course" needs?
- *Update friendly:* Regulations and requirements change, which may render old training manuals or videotapes inaccurate.
- *Assessment/Measurability:* It is important to ensure that all staff and physicians understand the materials and that there be a means of measuring the participation and impact of the training.

## External Lecture

Many organizations have found the lecture/course method of compliance training by an external professional to be beneficial. The credibility of the trainer in the eyes of the employees is likely to be high, and good trainers will have easily updateable material and should have strong assessment/measuring tools. Flexibility in scheduling may well be an issue, as may costs. The use of hypotheticals and case studies can drive messages home in a meaningful way, limit the risks of a "boring" lecture, and give the audience a chance to participate.

## Internal Lecture

Another option is for the organization's own compliance personnel to conduct the training in an internal lecture/course format. Despite the internal trainer's level of expertise, his or her perceived credibility is likely to be low. An internal lecture, however, would be reproducible, low in cost, and would be highly flexible, depending on the trainer's workload. Because an internal trainer would not be a training professional, he or she is unlikely to have experience with sensitive documentation issues or be able to easily update the relevant training.

## Lunch Meetings

Many organizations find that compliance related lunch meetings are a less formal, more relaxed means of presenting training topics. Lunch sessions offer significant advantages in terms of scheduling and flexibility. Frequently this will mean that there is no need to shut down the center, office, or department (with the inevitable loss of revenue) for a half- or full-day training session for all the physicians and office staff. Lunch sessions can be spread out over time and attendance staggered so that it is less disruptive. In many cases, the informal nature of a lunch program may make staff less defensive and more receptive to the training message.

As might be expected, there also are disadvantages with this approach. The use of frequent lunch sessions may mean that the choice of trainer is limited. Bringing in an expert from out of town is not cost-effective for a recurring lunch meeting; thus, the natural fit for this type of training is either an in-house trainer or, if possible, a local expert. Another disadvantage of conducting lunch sessions rather than full- or half-day lecture sessions would be the credibility challenge due to what some may perceive as a "lack of commitment" that may come with this approach. Further, trainee engagement may be low because lunch sessions may be too easy to skip or for employees to be called away to their "real" or "regular" duties.

## Computer-Based Training

As with everything else, this approach has advantages and disadvantages. Computer-based training is likely to have high perceived credibility from the trainees, with tremendous scheduling flexibility and reproducibility. In addition, many of the companies that provide computer-based training provide periodic updates, which is a significant benefit. Other factors to consider when looking at computer-based training include whether the module comes with assessment tools, and its ease of documentation.

The negatives of computer-based training include cost and focus. Computer-based training tends to be very expensive and is not usually able to be tailored to the specific needs and issues of your organization. For example, the training program you get on the computer may be one designed for all ambulatory surgery centers, not the specialty surgical center that you have.

## Words of Wisdom

As mentioned earlier, no single trainer or training approach is appropriate for every organization or situation. A "one size fits all" training component will lead to disaster—or at least a serious dose of frustration. It is important that organizations choose the approach that is determined to work best for them. Choosing the right training approach will entirely depend on an accurate assessment of your organization's needs.

# INDEX

legal issues in, 97–99, 101–103
vs. subcontracting, 69–70
refunds, of credit balances, 81–82,
89–90
relative value units (RVUs), of
multiple procedures, 13–14
renting space, 87–88, 107–108
research coverage, under
Medicare, 65–66
risk management, 37–73
Advanced Beneficiary Notices
for, 30, 37–38
advertising practice and, 47–48
carrier coding advice and,
39–40
clinical research coverage and,
65–66
colorectal cancer screening
and, 71–72
consultation definition and,
57–58
diagnosis coding and, 63–64
diagnostic test interpretation,
41–42
electronic records and, 73
Evaluation and Management
code guidelines, 43–45
medical necessity decisions
and, 67
Medicare utilization data use
for, 55–56
non-Medicare documentation
requirements and, 61–62
pharmaceutical company relationships and, 49–51
professional courtesy discounts
and, 53–54
screening vs. diagnostic
colonoscopy and, 59
subcontracting, 69–70
RVUs (multiple value units), of
multiple procedures, 13–14

safe harbors
for ambulatory surgery center
investments, 84–85
for leasing space, 108
for medical directorships,
105–106
screening colonoscopy, approval
of, 59, 71–72
scribe system, 9–10
sigmoidoscopy, flexible, Medicare
coverage of, 71–72
software
for claims processing, 3–4
vendors of, 113–114
Stark Law (Federal Physician
Anti-Self-Referral Law),
97–99, 101–103, 109–110
subcontractor services, billing for,
69–70
supervision requirements, 27,
101–103

technology, new, billing for, 29–30
telephone calls
billing for, 23–24
for carrier coding advice,
39–40
documentation of, 73
testimonials, in advertising, 47–48
training, for compliance, 127–128,
131–136
transfer of care, vs. consultation,
57–58
transportation services, for
patients, 93–95

usual charge, definition of, 19–20
utilization profiles, Medicare,
55–56

waste disposal, as laboratory servi-
ice, 115–116